Crisis Intervention Revisited

Revisited

A Guide to Modern Practice

Neil Thompson

Dedication: For Anna, David and Jenny

Acknowledgements

■ Special thanks are due to Ian Crompton, Training Officer, Cheshire Social Services, for contributing two of the case illustrations which form Chapter 5. Also, as my co-trainer in presenting courses on crisis intervention, Ian has played an important part in stimulating my thinking on the subject and has acted as a useful 'sounding board' for developing ideas.

■ I am indebted to the following people and agencies for providing information and/or advice in relation to the subject matter of Chapter 6:-

D A Wilkinson, Kent Social Services Department

A Robb, Grampian Social Work Department

Paul Walton, Sheffield Family and Community Services Department

Library and Information Officer, Nottinghamshire County Council

Policy and Information Section, Bradford Social Services Department

Sue Wilkinson, John Townsend and Spencer Webster, Cheshire Social Services Group

■ I am grateful to Colin Richardson, Fellow of Keele University, for his helpful comments and advice.

■ Thanks are due to Margaret More for typing the manuscript.

■ And, finally, I would not have been able to complete this book without the support of the special people in my life who have enabled me to cope with my own crises.

Neil Thompson   February 1991

The Author

Neil Thompson is a social work team leader with many years experience of crisis work in a social services setting. He is also a part-time social policy tutor with the Open University and completed his PhD on 'Existentialism and Social Work' at the University of Keele in 1989.

He is co-author (with Martina Osada and Bob Anderson) of 'Practice Teaching in Social Work: A Handbook', also published by PEPAR Publications.

Contents

Introduction

It has long been recognised that crises are a very important aspect of social work in particular and work with people in distress in general, e.g. health care. But just how important, indeed crucial, they can be is not always fully appreciated.

Crisis intervention is an approach which is premised on the argument that crises are fundamental and highly significant aspects of therapeutic work in a variety of settings and professions. Ignoring the nature, basis and implications of crisis is seen as dangerous, costly and detrimental to good professional practice. It is therefore essential to develop a clear and thorough understanding of crisis-related issues and learn the skills and techniques required to apply such concepts to one's practice with people in crisis. The facilitation of just such a process is precisely the aim of this book - a clear and concise introduction to the theory and methods of crisis intervention and the advantages and difficulties associated with adopting such an approach.

The emphasis is strongly on crisis intervention as an applied method. This is neither purely a theoretical treatise nor simply an atheoretical 'commonsense' guide to practice. It is intended as a bridge between theory and practice - a study which takes account of both of these important dimensions and the interaction between the two.

I shall be using the term 'crisis' in a slightly technical sense but the meaning ascribed to it is not very far removed from the everyday 'commonsense' usage of the word. This should become clearer in the pages that follow.

A crisis is a turning point, a situation which pushes our usual coping mechanisms beyond their limits of effectiveness and thus necessitates a different response, a different strategy for coping.

The term 'crisis' is often used in everyday speech to denote a highly stressful or traumatic situation or set of circumstances. However, this rather loose usage of the term is unhelpful, for we need to be precise about what we mean by 'crisis'. The amount of stress, quantitatively speaking, is not necessarily an indicator of crisis. For example, a student may feel considerable stress and pressure when facing exams but may nonetheless cope quite effectively without having to take drastic steps. In other words he/she may take it in his/her stride and thus, despite the high level of stress and pressure, a crisis does not arise. For others, however, who may not be so well-equipped to handle such stress, a crisis may be provoked by an even lower level of stress. 'Crisis' is therefore a qualitative concept rather than simply a quantitative one.

The issues relating to coping abilities, how and why they break down and the consequences of such breakdown will be consistent themes throughout this text. They are key aspects of crisis intervention, for it is in relation to these factors that intervention by a skilled helper can be so fruitful, as indeed we shall see below. Crisis is the 'critical' moment, the time when significant changes can be made as a result of the energy and motivation the situation produces. These changes can prove to be constructive or destructive, helpful or detrimental and so crisis point is very much a turning point, simultaneously a threat and an opportunity for growth. It is a challenge. It has challenged and defeated the coping mechanisms within one's usual repertoire and is now challenging one's ability to develop new and effective methods of handling the situation. One of the key roles for the therapist in crisis intervention is therefore an educative one, to teach people in crisis new and effective responses, to guide them towards positive and constructive use of crisis.

Very often the response of those close to a person in crisis is to look for a shortcut through the crisis or simply to sit it out. This is often mistakenly referred to as crisis intervention but this type of 'patching up' of a crisis would be more accurately termed 'crisis survival' as the aim is to minimise damage rather than maximise therapeutic potential.

Crisis intervention does not therefore simply mean intervening in crises; it is a specific approach to crisis based on a set of theoretical principles, a conceptual framework to guide and inform practice. This book should not therefore be seen as a study of crisis as a general phenomenon but rather an introduction to the specific concepts and techniques which are of value to those workers in the health and welfare fields who are called upon to deal with crises.

Chapter 1 presents a brief and schematic account of traditional crisis theory and its key tenets. It also attempts, albeit in outline only, to indicate some weakpoints of the traditional thinking on the subject and to point to a more sophisticated and updated theoretical basis.

Chapter 2 is in two parts, both of which address the positive use of crisis, the potential for learning and growth inherent in the challenge of crisis. The first part begins with an analysis of the physiological concomitants of crisis and from this moves on to examine the usefulness of assertiveness training. The second part discusses the relevance and applicability of social learning theory and offers guidance on the use of appropriate techniques.

Chapter 3 emphasises the need for quick, clear and accurate assessment and explores some of the skills required and how they can be developed.

Chapter 4 tackles the issues of putting theory into practice - the 'nuts and bolts' of intervention, as it were. This chapter attempts to paint a picture of what a crisis intervention approach in action actually looks like.

Chapter 5 provides illustrations of the themes and issues so far raised. Three case studies based on actual examples of crisis intervention practice within a social work context are presented. Links are drawn between the practice situations and the theoretical issues which underpin them.

Chapter 6 examines the use of crisis theory in disaster situations such as Hillsborough, Piper Alpha or Zeebrugge. The similarities and differences between individual/familial crisis work and large-scale disaster work are examined.

Chapter 7 is the concluding chapter. As well as restating the main themes and drawing the discussion to a close this chapter raises questions about the support networks needed and the agency implications for workers who seek to adopt a crisis intervention approach.

The message I seek to convey in this text is that crisis intervention is a very useful and effective theory-based approach to helping people deal positively with a wide range of potentially destructive crisis situations. It is a very demanding approach, but the case I wish to argue here, on the basis of many years experience of using these methods, is that the benefits of this approach far outweigh the costs in terms of time, energy and emotional commitment.

Hopefully, the following chapters will succeed in clarifying and justifying our faith in crisis intervention.

Chapter 1

Crisis Theory: Old and New

The theoretical underpinnings of crisis intervention are based on a 'problem-solving' model of human functioning and learning. Each day we are faced with a range of problems to solve, mostly of a minor nature. In order to cope with this procession of problems we develop a range of coping responses which are variously known as 'mechanisms', 'skills', 'methods', or 'strategies'. This repertoire includes interpersonal skills, stress management techniques and other forms of practical and emotional resourcefulness.

There are two basic dimensions to this process of dealing with problems - the subjective and the objective. The objective element consists of the external factors which go to make up the problem situation - the personal, social and economic circumstances of those involved. The subjective element relates to the 'inner state' of the person(s) concerned - the perceptions, emotions and cognitive processes which contribute to, and respond to, the objective circumstances. Crisis theory makes it clear that the subjective is not simply a reflection of the objective as if some mechanistic or deterministic process were operating. The relationship between the subjective and the objective is based on a range of complex psychological and social interactions. The details of this need not concern us here but the key point from a crisis theory point of view is that dealing with problems has both a subjective and objective dimension and consequently the breakdown of coping mechanisms and subsequent development of new coping methods can relate to either or both dimensions. It is a mistake, both theoretically and therapeutically, to concentrate on one at the expense of the other.

As was argued earlier, in the introduction, a crisis is qualitatively different from 'problems' in the wider sense. A crisis necessarily involves change or movement for, by definition, conventional 'tactics' have failed or proven inappropriate. Such change can be positive or negative, deterioration or improvement, damage or progress. (This theme will be explored more fully in Chapter 2 below.) Consequently crisis is characterised by risk and hence tension and anxiety. Such risk and the challenges it entails are therefore important aspects and a practitioner who fails to recognise this may do more harm than good, for his/her intervention also becomes part of the crisis scenario. Practitioners using crisis intervention need to be sensitive to the risks involved and be ready to intervene, where necessary, in maximising the positive potential of the situation.

In order to undertake this task, an understanding of the characteristics of crisis is needed and it is to this that we now turn.

One of the central concepts relating to crisis is that of loss. Lindemann's study of grief reactions outlined the main responses to a serious loss. From a detailed study of 101 bereaved relatives he detected a pattern consisting largely of the following elements (See Lindemann, 1944, 1965):-

1. Somatic distress - physical symptoms, e.g. nausea, debility.

2. Preoccupation with the deceased's image - a tendency to focus on images or matters relating to the person lost.

3. Guilt - self blame, however irrational, in relation to the death or prior circumstances.

4. Hostile reactions - anger directed at others, whether justified or not.

5. Loss of patterns of conduct - temporary disruption of usual behaviour.

6. Adopting traits of the deceased person - taking on some of the mannerisms or personality characteristics of the person lost.

These reactions were deemed to be 'normal' or 'healthy' insofar as they lead to a successful resolution of the situation without harm to the individual's psychological or social functioning. They are characteristics of successful crisis management.

There are, however, other grief reactions which are deemed to be 'morbid' or 'pathological'; that is, they may be indicative of a crisis being handled in a harmful or unsuccessful way. These are:-

1. Postponed reaction - no immediate reaction but may surface later at an unexpected or inappropriate time.

2. Accumulative reactions - where the grieving process is delayed or restricted, the negative effects will be cumulative if a further loss is experienced.

3. Overactivity - especially in relation to the deceased.

4. Development of symptoms - especially those associated with the illness of the deceased.

5. Stress-related illness - ulcerative colitis, asthma or psychosomatic reactions.

6. Disruption of social relationships - avoidance of people or irritation with them.

7. Hostility - even towards people who have helped.

8. Loss of affect - flattening of emotions, feelings of 'nothing matters'.

9. Disruption of patterns of interaction - indecision, inactivity, constant need for prompting.

10. Detrimental activities - extreme generosity, theft.

11. Agitated depression - feelings of worthlessness and bitterness. (See Parad, 1965, p8ff)

It should be noted that these were identified as potentially problematic and did not automatically indicate 'pathology', to use Lindemann's term. They are to be seen as 'warning signs' of potential problems rather than clear 'symptoms' of a failure to grieve effectively.

From this understanding of the crisis of bereavement, a tradition of crisis theory developed with major steps made in the 1960's (Caplan, 1961, Langsley and Kaplan, 1968.) Lindemann's ideas were generalised to other forms of loss - for example, loss of job, status, self-esteem, health, or loss through divorce etc. On the basis of clinical findings, it was theorised that a standard pattern of grief reaction is to be found in all crises. Loss and the concomitant grief reactions are therefore key aspects of crisis theory. It is for this reason that crisis work is sometimes referred to as 'loss counselling'.

Caplan (1961) sees crises as having three distinct phases as follows:-

1. The Impact Stage

This initial stage is characterised by stress and confusion and a sense of disbelief. The situation seems unreal. Comments such as "I can't believe it's happened" or "It hasn't sunk in yet" are not uncommon. Profound feelings of emptiness, loss and disorientation are experienced.

2. The Recoil Stage

This first stage is relatively short-lived and quickly leads on to 'the recoil stage' which is characterised by disorganisation and intensity of emotion. This emotion can be directed outwards as anger or inwards as guilt, or indeed both simultaneously. The disorganisation common at this stage can lead to incompetence, e.g. in using machinery or driving. Physical symptoms can also feature at this stage of the crisis process, e.g. fatigue, headaches, stomach disorder.

3. Adjustment and Adaptation

The crisis literature contains differing estimates of the time-scale of the crisis process but most fall within a 4 to 8 week framework. The adjustment and adaptation stage is therefore reached in a relatively short period. It is the 'exit' stage of the crisis for it is at this point that the success or failure of the crisis resolution will be determined. This is the stage of 'breakthrough or breakdown'. The situation is resolved to a greater or lesser extent as the available coping resources are mobilised. Breakthrough occurs when new and effective coping methods are learned or new sources of support are discovered or created. Breakdown occurs when an inappropriate or ineffective method is used, for in such circumstances this is likely to provoke a further crisis in which the coping resources will be further challenged. This is the time at which skilled intervention can be crucial. It can mean the difference between breakthrough and breakdown.

The worker's task within crisis intervention can therefore be seen as helping the person(s) in crisis to develop new and effective coping mechanisms. When such learning is achieved, the people concerned grow stronger as they are now better equipped to cope with the next crisis when it comes. And the next crisis surely will come, as crises, whether major or minor, are a basic part of everyday life.

Such crises are of two basic types, situational and maturational. The latter are the 'life-crises' of developmental psychology - adolescence, parenthood, the menopause, etc. There is a certain, albeit limited, predictability associated with these crises - they follow a certain pattern or regularity (see Erikson, 1977). Situational crises, by contrast, are relatively individualised and unpredictable - they depend very much on personal circumstances.

Whatever the type of crisis, there should be an identifiable 'precipitant event', the response to which is the commencement of the crisis. The 'precipitant event' can be seen as the objective dimension while the 'precipitant' is the subjective response to that event. The subjective dimension is primary, for an event not perceived as a crisis will not be experienced as a crisis. For example, while one person may be plunged into crisis by a road traffic accident, others may not as they are able to take such matters in their stride - they are better equipped in terms of coping resources. Such resources consist of skills and coping strategies developed by previous experience, together with wider social and economic resources. Traditional crisis theory can be criticised for emphasising the former at the expense of the latter but we shall return to this point below.

Precipitating factors are important aspects of the 'aetiology' of crisis but Getz et al (1974) argue that it is not necessary to know what precipitated the crisis. The precise details are not needed for intervention to be effective and this is indeed consistent with a further principle of crisis intervention, that of future-orientation.

When a crisis is encountered, feelings of not coping are experienced and the question arises: how am I going to cope in future? The future is therefore an important dimension and crisis theory posits that intervention should consequently be future-oriented. This is a significant departure from other therapeutic schools of thought such as psychodynamics and behaviourism which focus on the significance of the past. Crises often produce a tendency to dwell on past failures, whereas the positive thrust of crisis intervention seeks to concentrate on future successes by developing new coping mechanisms - and thus reintroduce hope. In simple terms, crisis theory argues that there is no point 'crying over spilled milk' and instead, the energy generated by the crisis should be channelled positively towards the future.

A key concept within the crisis theory framework is that of 'homeostasis', the ability to maintain control of one's emotions and to cope with one's personal circumstances. It refers to a balanced state in which everyday problems are met with and overcome by our usual repertoire of coping methods. In short, it is precisely a state of 'non-crisis', a psychological equilibrium. It is not necessarily a happy state as it can be very stressful, but the point is that the balance is maintained without serious challenge to the individual. When homeostasis breaks down, crisis begins. Ewing (1978) expresses this as follows:-

"The individual is continually confronted with situations that threaten to upset the consistent pattern and balance of his emotional functioning... Sometimes, however, the threatening situation is of such magnitude that it cannot be readily mastered by habitual methods of problem-solving. It is then, says Caplan, that the individual begins to experience 'crisis'." (pp 12-13)

There is, as Ewing goes on to say, an imbalance between the perceived threat and the resources available for coping. The distorted form of crisis intervention to which we referred in the introduction as 'crisis survival' would simply seek to restore homeostasis as soon as possible whereas crisis intervention proper seeks to use the crisis to develop new and better ways of coping - to empower the client. The effect of this development is to extend and strengthen the coping repertoire and thus reduce the risk of further crises. In this respect, crisis survival tends to produce dependency, for an inappropriately resolved crisis is likely to produce a new crisis but leaving those concerned feeling weakened, rather than strengthened, by the initial crisis. Crisis intervention, by contrast, discourages dependency by teaching people how to cope, strengthening and empowering them so that their independence is promoted.

This is a significant practice implication of crisis theory and there are indeed many such implications. These will be the topic of Chapter 4 and will also be relevant to Chapters 2 and 3.

This, then is a very cursory introduction to traditional crisis theory but before moving on to examine how these ideas can be realised in practice, let us first pinpoint a number of criticisms and how the theory can be modified and extended to take account of them.

One significant weakness apparent in the crisis intervention approach is its relative overemphasis on 'internal' psychological coping resources and underemphasis on wider social or community resources for coping. A crisis can be an opportunity not only for developing coping skills or psychological mechanisms but also for discovering or cultivating other sources of support or assistance within the local community or the wider social sphere, for example a self-help group. The crisis literature does acknowledge and refer to such 'external' sources but tends to gloss over them as the main focus is clearly a clinical one geared towards traditional psychological issues. The wider social issues are therefore paid inadequate attention.

A more balanced crisis theory would need to develop a fuller analysis of the role and significance of wider support systems in the prevention or resolution of crises. A more sophisticated model would present the interplay of personal and social forces as well as the interplay of subjective and objective factors. This can be represented schematically as follows:-

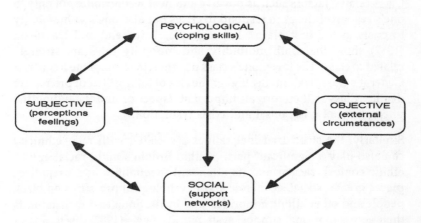

Although there are only four elements within this matrix, it is clear that it already produces a complex set of interactions. The traditional emphasis on the psychological level only therefore presents a rather distorted picture of the situation.

Similarly, the level of explanation of traditional crisis theory is an individual or, at best, familial one. Kieran O'Hagan (1986) criticises the 'pioneers' for failing to appreciate the family context of crisis

13

situations. However, his own solution - the advocacy of a crisis intervention based on family therapy - makes the same mistake, that of ignoring its own context, this time the structural context. How well equipped a person is to deal with a crisis depends upon not only psychological factors, not only family dynamics but also structural social divisions such as class, race and gender (see, for example, Jones, 1983, Dominelli, 1988, Hanmer and Statham, 1988).

Power and opportunities ('life-chances' as Weber called them) are not randomly distributed within society but are clearly linked to the structure of society. Class is a reflection of socio-economic position and this is, of course, a significant issue in relation to the availability of coping resources. Wealth and economic power do not guarantee an absence of crisis, far from it, but money can buy access to wider coping resources (e.g. the services of a solicitor, private medicine, expensive holidays to relieve stress, etc.) Access to resources in general can therefore be seen to parallel access to coping resources in particular.

Class-related factors such as poverty and health contribute not only to one's resourcefulness to respond to crises but also one's vulnerability to crisis in the first place. For example, Townsend and Davidson (1987) show that both morbidity and mortality rates are strongly related to class. The lower one's class position (in terms of the Registrar-General's classification) the higher the risk of falling ill or of premature death. Class is therefore an important aspect of understanding the phenomena of crisis onset and crisis resolution.

Similarly, the structured inequalities associated with race/ethnicity can also play a significant part. Within Britain's multi-racial, multi-ethnic context, racism and its attendant inequalities and prejudices places greater social, economic and psychological pressures on black people and other ethnic minorities, and institutionalised racism limits their access to formal support systems. Rooney's (1987) discussion of the under-representation of black people in the provision of social services resources provides good examples of the way implicit discrimination is so often 'built-in' to social work structures and institutions.

Race and ethnicity should therefore be recognised as important aspects of the 'crisis matrix', the complex web of factors which contribute to the crisis scenario. Racism can be seen as a contributory factor in both the onset of crisis, as a result of the stresses and pressures[1] it brings to bear, and the resolution of crisis, in terms of restricted access to institutional support networks.

Similarly, inequalities based on gender place an increased burden of coping on women. For example, as Finch and Groves (1983) point out, women are expected to be the main providers of care for children, elderly or disabled relatives, etc. Thus Finch and Groves argue that community care is in fact family care which, in turn, amounts primarily to care by women. The burden of coping placed on women's shoulders is therefore a very heavy one.

This is only one example amongst many of extra pressures upon women as a result of the patriarchal ideology which operates in modern British society (see, for example Mayes, 1986). Thus, women may be more vulnerable to crisis due to the oppressive nature of a society based on sexism. Ettorre (1989), for example, links women's substance abuse (both illegal drugs and tranquillisers etc.) to the socially constructed dependency role women are expected to occupy. She comments:-

> "... tranquilliser use in the private sphere may be, whether consciously or not, a housewife's only comfort and relief from stress." (1989, p107)

Also, there is a significant body of research, for example Brown and Harris (1978), which establishes links between women and depression. Factors such as lack of outlet for the domestic sphere, relative isolation and lack of emotional support were found to be strongly associated with depression and these, in turn, are associated with the circumstances of women in modern Britain

In sum, therefore, traditional crisis theory can be criticised for adopting a predominantly white, middle-class, male perspective on a range of issues which relate very closely to structured inequalities and the oppressive social divisions which stack the odds against certain groups in society. An understanding of social disadvantage and discrimination must be incorporated into the theoretical framework if a new crisis

---

(1) For example, the fact that black youth receive more than their fair share of negative attention within the criminal justice system, (Whitehouse, 1986)

theory is to replace the old and thereby make a contribution to anti-discriminatory practice.

Furthermore, the major social divisions of class, race and gender are not the only ones which need to be considered. Age, disability and sexual orientation are also relevant factors as indeed are any other forms of discrimination and disadvantage.

One of the main reasons for traditional crisis theory's blindness to these structural factors is the model of society which it uses as its baseline, namely what sociologists would call a 'consensus' model. This model assumes that there are no fundamental conflicts of interest within society and that whatever conflicts do occur are peripheral to the underlying consensus of what is presented as a basically homogeneous society. This somewhat naive model needs to be replaced with a more sophisticated 'conflict' one which addresses, and takes account of, the conflicts of class, race and gender etc., which are part and parcel of the structure of society, for such conflicts circumscribe the situations in which crises occur and structure the coping resources available and are thus important dimensions of crisis intervention.

Another major weakness of crisis intervention which flows from this consensus model is its use of the now somewhat outmoded notion of 'adjustment'. Words such as 'maladaptive' are frequently employed to indicate unsuccessful or unhelpful behaviours. This is suggestive of someone who fails to fit in with social expectations, someone who is unable or unwilling to conform to standardised views of appropriate behaviour. The problem with this notion is that it 'pathologises' the person(s) concerned. It implies that the problem underlying the crisis is a 'failure of adjustment' and thus lays the blame for the situation on the individual(s) experiencing the crisis. This is a 'reductionist' approach insofar as it reduces a complex socio-psychological situation to a straightforward matter of pathology, of individual failing.

Clearly this involves a value judgment which could act as a barrier to therapeutic progress. A more appropriate and less judgmental concept is that of 'empowerment'. The task of the crisis worker is to empower people to take greater control of their circumstances and thus be better equipped to handle future crises - to be in a more powerful position. The notion of 'adjustment' implies that changes need to be internal, psychological ones whereas empowerment is a more global concept, encompassing both internal, personal power (e.g. control of emotions, ability to resist panic) and wider power issues relating to social circumstances (e.g. a woman obtaining an injunction against a violent partner).

If the crisis worker is to seek empowerment rather than adjustment, this entails not simply counselling geared towards coping skills but also advocacy and other such ways of tackling the 'external' as well as internal factors (Thompson, 1989). This involves taking a wider perspective than a clinical casework approach and thus taking account of social, as well as individual or familial factors.

The wider the focus the worker takes, the smaller the impact he or she can have upon the factors identified. The narrower, more individualistic the focus, the greater the impact the worker can have in terms of power, influence and access to resources. This, however, should not be used as an excuse for not attempting to influence or change the wider social issues.

In addition to the structural dimension neglected by the early theorists, Nira Kfir introduces a further dimension paid insufficient attention by the 'pioneers', namely the relevance of existential issues to an understanding of crisis (Seligson, 1987).

As a rule, questions about the purpose and meaning of life are rarely addressed. Within the complacency of homeostasis we take such matters for granted and, if they do arise, they are usually dismissed by jokes about 'the meaning of life' etc. However, at a time of crisis, such issues tend to loom large. Feelings of loneliness, emptiness and meaninglessness are characteristic of crisis as it is, in effect, an existential experience insofar as it replaces the security of homeostasis with doubt and existential uncertainty. Seligson comments:-

> "In crisis, the person feels that there is no future, therefore they have no goals and hence no meaning in life. Only that person in crisis knows when the meaning of his life collapses. This is the essential existential loneliness of the crisis situation. Everything is nothing." (1987, p77)

Indeed, crisis theory owes much to existentialism with its emphasis on the interplay of subjective and objective factors, unpredictability and uncertainty and the need to take positive control of one's life (see Sartre, 1958, Barnes, 1974).

Existentialism stresses the importance of choices, of the decisions we make and the consequences which flow from these, both in personal and social terms, individual and collective. Such decisions are characterised by risk and contingency and so the potential for losing control and entering crisis is an everpresent one and therefore something we need to learn to come to terms with. Rollo May, an existentialist psychotherapist comments:-

> "Existentialism is an attitude which accepts man as always becoming, which means potentially in crisis."
> (May et al, 1958 p86)

Whilst existentialism is an influential school of thought in psychotherapy, its status and influence in social work is of a much lower order. However, to maximise our understanding of crises and appropriate interventions, a fuller understanding of the existential aspects should be high on the agenda.

Traditional crisis theory is premised on the ego-psychology of writers such as Erikson (1977) but what is hopefully now clear is that such a theoretical basis is inadequate and needs to be extended in a number of ways. O'Hagan (1986) recognises some of the weaknesses, castigates the 'pioneers' for their narrow, psychiatric focus and proposes family systems theory as an improvement. However, as mentioned earlier, this does not go far enough. It neglects the structural and existential dimensions, both of which have significant and far-reaching implications for theory, practice and policy.

The flaws apparent within crisis theory are major ones but, having acknowledged this, we should beware the danger of 'throwing the baby out with the bath water', by rejecting crisis intervention as an inappropriate or outmoded approach to dealing with people in distress.

Much work needs to be done to strengthen the theoretical basis of crisis work so that it can provide a more adequate knowledge base to guide practice. However, what also needs to be achieved - and here I am in agreement with O'Hagan - is the development of practice skills, the actual 'nuts and bolts' of dealing effectively and constructively with people experiencing disabling crises. The development of theory is therefore not an end in itself but rather a means to an end. That end is the establishment of high quality professional practice, based on crisis intervention principles.

To conclude this introductory chapter on the theory-base of crisis intervention, let me summarise, in diagram form, the theoretical developments I see as necessary for the revitalisation of crisis intervention as a major approach to social work.

Crisis Theory

Old	New
Psychology	Psychology and Sociology
Adjustment	Empowerment
Consensus	Conflict
Family context	Social-structural context:-
	class
	race/ethnicity
	gender
	age etc.
Focus on individual	Holistic focus (including individual/family)
Internal	Internal and external
No specific philosophical basis	Existentialist basis
Pathological	Socio-psychological
Personal resources	Personal and social resources

What I seek to do, therefore, is to build upon the sound foundations of early crisis theory but, in so doing, discard those aspects which are inappropriate to modern day social work and replace them with more relevant and less restricted concepts, which thus gives us a much stronger framework for intervention.

Chapter 2

The Positive Dimension of Crisis

A crisis is a turning point, a time of decision in which a prior state of equilibrium has been disturbed. The result of this can be either positive or negative - one's capacity to cope with future problems, stresses and crises can be enhanced or diminished.

As Aguilera and Messick (1986) point out, the Chinese character representing 'crisis' means both opportunity and danger. This captures well the positive potential of crisis together with the significant risk of harm, whether this be physical, emotional or social. The intervention of the crisis worker can be crucial in determining which way the outcome of the crisis falls - positive or negative.

The crisis situation produces a biological stress response as the 'fight or flight' mechanism is activated. The body responds by releasing adrenalin and thereby producing extra energy and thus motivation. The physical concomitants of crisis are manifold - higher pulse rate, dry mouth, 'butterflies' sensation etc. These are the bodily manifestations of feelings of anxiety, threat or loss.

However, when we consider the bodily response to feelings of joy, exhilaration or celebration, we can detect strong, if not exact, parallels with the stress response. The body responds to both stress and excitement in basically the same way, that is by entering a 'state of arousal'. It is this state of arousal which the crisis worker can use to the full in attempting to realise a positive outcome from the crisis by exploiting the energy and motivation generated.

This state is known in acting circles as the 'buzz', that state of nervous excitement which can either inhibit or inspire. Drama teaching involves learning to control this 'buzz' and use it as a positive tool. Similarly, assertiveness training involves attempting to harness the strong feelings produced by situations of conflict or potential confrontation and use them in a positive and constructive way.

At a biological, bodily level, the sensations experienced in extreme situations are the same, regardless of whether it is a positive or negative extreme. It is at the psychological, rather than the physical level that we distinguish between the two extremes, between joy and fear. The body's response is a recognition of an unusual, extraordinary situation or, to use the jargon, a breakdown of homeostasis. In this sense, an extreme situation of joy can be a crisis, with both danger and opportunity present. An example of how such a crisis can 'go wrong' is that of the 'spend, spend, spend' problems of some football pools winners, the breakdown of their normal coping mechanisms and psychologically important sense of equilibrium. (There is a significant overlap here with Durkheim's concept of 'anomie', Durkheim, 1952.)

The physical sensations are the objective dimension, but we must also acknowledge the subjective dimension - the interpretation of such sensations. How we interpret these will depend very much on the circumstances of their occurrence in relation to the goals and values we have adopted (and this in turn depends on our 'social location' in terms of such social dimensions as class, race, gender, age etc.) And this is where the positive use of crisis comes to the fore, for it is possible for us to alter our goals or values if the circumstances dictate. This is known as 'cognitive restructuring' and is a common way of coping with stress. For example, if I fail an exam or fail to get a job I applied for, one way of coping with the negative feelings is to change direction, to develop a different ambition or aspiration.

The task of the crisis worker may therefore be to help the person(s) in crisis review or renegotiate certain aspects of their thoughts, feelings or intentions. This, of course, is not as simple as it may initially sound but the positive potential is nonetheless there. In the same way that there is nothing inherently good or bad about the bodily response to crisis - it is 'neutral' - there is nothing inherently good or bad about the psychological response to the situation - it all depends on how we deal with it. Crisis intervention, and this is the crux, is geared towards helping people maximise the positive potential by dealing effectively with the 'crisis matrix', the various aspects of the crisis situation, and thus exploiting the learning opportunities.

Within crisis theory, the term 'crisis' is not to be equated with the commonsense usage in the sense of a 'disaster', for this necessarily entails a negative conclusion. A crisis, in this technical sense, is potentially negative or positive and I shall discuss below some of the ways in which the balance can be tilted towards the positive.

To illustrate this further, let us consider the different levels of coping and a 'chart' of how these can be affected by crisis.

Each of us has a characteristic 'level of functioning' in terms of our ability to deal with the range of problems we encounter in our day to day circumstances. This 'normal' level of functioning is that of homeostasis. Crisis occurs, by definition, when this homeostatic level of equilibrium is upset. Equilibrium will eventually be restored but it may be at a different level. This new level could be lower, in which case the crisis can be seen to have attacked and reduced our coping abilities. For example, a court appearance may leave someone with little or no pride or confidence and therefore that person is less well-equipped to deal with other problems and challenges as and when they arise. The same precipitant event, a court appearance, may, by contrast, be a significant turning point in a positive way. It may give a strong determination to steer clear of potential law-breaking and take a more controlled, less aimless, approach to one's life and thus produce more effective coping skills and a higher level of functioning.

The outcome level is therefore variable, depending upon the response of the person(s) in crisis and, where applicable, the crisis worker(s). These different levels can be represented diagrammatically as follows:-

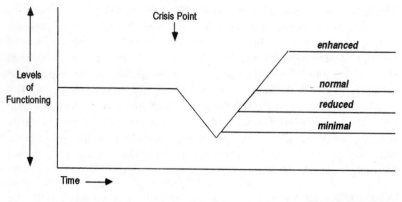

(Based on Hill, 1965)

Crisis inevitably produces a lowering of coping ability on a temporary basis as we pass through the impact and recoil phases. However to what level it returns in the exit phase is not predictable, as it depends so much on the actions of those involved.

In order to ensure, as far as possible, that the outcome is a beneficial one [1] in terms of an enhanced level of functioning, steps must be taken to minimise the danger element and concentrate on the opportunity element. This is the basis of crisis intervention and can be achieved in a number of ways, for example:-

1. Mobilise appropriate support system resources, e.g. by advocacy.

2. Through rapport and positive interest, offer the person(s) in crisis a degree of calming reassurance and a temporary prop to their self-esteem and confidence.

3. Facilitate the learning of new and more effective coping mechanisms e.g. by counselling.

These issues will be addressed more fully in Chapter 4, but it is worth noting at this stage that such forms of intervention play a significant role in the positive use of crisis. This is to be distinguished, as indeed it was earlier, from 'crisis survival' which seeks to restore homeostasis as *quickly* as possible rather than as *constructively* as possible.

A further point which needs to be emphasised is that we should not confuse the positive use of crisis with a strategy of provoking crisis as part of one's therapeutic work. It should be remembered that crisis represents not only opportunity but also danger. Deliberately provoking a crisis, albeit in a well-intentioned way as part of an overall strategy, may nonetheless result in considerable harm to vulnerable people. The ethics of such an approach are very questionable indeed. Crisis intervention entails capitalising on crises - making the best of a bad job, as it were - but this is very different from *causing* a crisis. This point has often been misunderstood and crisis intervention has therefore attracted inappropriate and inaccurate criticism.

Let us now move on to examine the positive dimension of crisis from a different angle. We have identified that learning and the facilitation of learning are key aspects of crisis intervention. There is a theoretical perspective which combines the positive dimension with learning, namely social learning theory.

---

(1) The precipitant event may be anything but positive, for example the death of a loved one, but the ensuing crisis may have positive implications in terms of enhancing one's future ability to cope.

The following outline of the theory, and its applicability to crisis situations, continues the theme of the positive dimension, but also sets the scene for Chapter 4's topic, the use of crisis theory in practice - the process of intervention.

If we recap briefly on Caplan's model of crisis, it helps us examine our positive role in terms of client intervention. The ultimate goal of any counsellor dealing with clients with crises is to teach new and better coping skills or facilitate in whatever ways possible the development of these. In other words, they come out of crisis with more ability to cope when similar experiences occur in the future. In order to be able to teach these skills we need to be aware of how people learn new behaviour. This is where social learning theory comes into the picture.

Starting from infancy, we build up our learned behaviour according to how much it is encouraged. Social learning theory teaches us that behaviour is learned from the environment and from the effect created on the environment by our actions. That is, there is an interplay between the effects of the environment upon our actions and of our actions upon the environment. (This is parallel to the dialectic of subjectivity and objectivity discussed in Chapter 1). An example of this would be a child who, given attention as a result of crying, learns that crying is an effective way of gaining attention and thus further similar incidents of crying are encouraged. The response of other people to the behaviour is therefore significant in influencing the likelihood of the behaviour continuing or being repeated. As we shall see, the environment consists of multiple influences and these change according to time and place.

One of the key concepts of this theory is that of *reinforcement*, a process we saw in operation in the 'crying' example above. Most consequences of behaviour can be thought of as resting along a line or dimension from pleasant to unpleasant as shown diagrammatically below:-

pleasant — — — — — — — — — — — — — — unpleasant

This continuum is used to show that not all pleasant experiences are of equal effect. Even the same one may vary in its effect according to time, place or the influence of other factors.

The closer an experience is to the 'pleasant' pole, the more likely is its reoccurrence as the behaviour which produced the pleasant experience will thus be encouraged or 'reinforced'. That is, in general, behaviours that result in pleasant effects are likely to be increased. Positive consequences are said to *reinforce* behaviour, that is they will increase the chances of the behaviour happening again.

This far, the ideas presented here will be familiar to many social workers or others involved in counselling/supportive work, although it is perhaps questionable whether the concept is fully utilised in practice. In order to use reinforcement as part of a therapeutic repertoire, we need to see it in the wider context of social learning theory.

The theory argues that behaviour is maximally increased when reinforcement is:

> *sufficient*
> *immediate*
> *consistent.*

1. As argued above, the more pleasant an experience is, the stronger the reinforcement will be.

2. The greater the length of time between a behaviour and its positive consequences, the weaker the reinforcement will be. It therefore pays to keep the time gap to a minimum, to make the reinforcement as immediate as possible.

3. The more consistently a behaviour is rewarded by positive consequences, the greater the likelihood of its recurrence. However, set against this is the principle of *intermittent* reinforcement. Once behaviour is established, it is best 'kept going' by occasional or 'intermittent' reinforcement rather than by regular reinforcement, (see Rachlin, 1976) for example, teaching a dog to sit.

These are therefore three key principles of behavioural learning and, as such, are important aspects of facilitating and promoting the learning of new skills.

These are not the only tenets of social learning theory of value but space does not permit a more detailed analysis.

In the absence of reinforcement, behaviour tends to decrease or even stop. This is known as 'extinguishing'. It is therefore clear that the counsellor can play a significant role in either promoting the positive reinforcement of helpful and constructive behaviours or contributing to the extinction of negative or harmful behaviours by removing, preventing or discouraging reinforcement. For example, where a client lacks self-esteem, confidence-boosting behaviours can be promoted and self-denigrating behaviours can be discouraged. However, a strong note of caution needs to be made here. In such a position the counsellor has considerable power and influence over the client in terms of defining what is positive and what is negative, as these are clearly value judgments. This point will be addressed again in the conclusion below (Chapter 7), but we should note that the ethics of using a behavioural approach have often been questioned (see Sheldon, 1982).

But how, you may be asking, does social learning theory relate to crisis work? Firstly, it is important, in order to engage the client, that areas of coping in a person's life are reinforced in order that such behaviours are maintained as far as possible through and beyond the crisis situation. For example, in dealing with a case of alcohol misuse on a man's part, his partner may have done extremely well in clothing and feeding their child even though most of the family income may have been spent on alcohol. It is important that such coping strengths are recognised

a) to boost confidence and promote a positive, coping attitude, and

b) to build a positive therapeutic rapport, i.e. to 'engage' the client.

Secondly, as we shall discuss in Chapter 3, clear and accurate assessment is a key part of crisis intervention. Identifying which behaviours are to be reinforced and developed and which to be extinguished is a significant component of the assessment process.

Thirdly, if we are indeed to make positive use of crisis, it is very important that appropriate changes in behaviour, however small, are reinforced by the counsellor or significant others. The aim of this is to foster the growth of new coping methods and nurture a positive and self-directing frame of mind.

A further dimension of social learning theory which is of very direct and significant relevance to crisis intervention is that of goal-setting.

From the beginning of our intervention, goal-setting will be important in order to give a framework to the work done with the client. One of the characteristics of crisis is a feeling of loss of control, a lack of structure and therefore a sense of meaninglessness and alienation. It is therefore important to re-establish the parameters, to create a new and meaningful framework. Goal-setting is an important area of social learning theory work which helps to build a helpful structured framework.

Goal-setting is based on positive achievement and should be a process worked out between client and worker. It is not enough for the worker to impose his/her own goals (indeed it can be positively harmful to do so) as the aim is not simply to help the client survive the crisis but rather to learn from this crisis in order to cope better with future demands and potential and actual crises. There is also the issue of the potential for abuse of the power the worker has over the client who is vulnerable by virtue of his/her crisis state, as mentioned earlier in this chapter. It is therefore vital to work *with* the client in terms of goals, although it should be noted that the pressure of a crisis can make it a strong temptation to work at your own pace and in your own direction.

In general, it is to be emphasised that goals should be *short-term* and *incremental*. In the intense emotional 'heat' of a crisis, the time-scale is very telescoped and so long-term goals have little meaning in such situations. Also, it is important for people in crisis to develop a sense of 'progress', a sense that they are gradually regaining their equilibrium. The incremental nature of goal-setting is therefore highly appropriate to this task of instilling a sense of progress.

It is far better to have a series of short-term goals rather than one major long-term goal, although there is, of course, always the one major long-term aim, that of enhancing the client's problem-solving and coping methods.

In setting goals, it should be remembered that these should be reasonably easy to achieve. This is for two reasons, as follows:-

1. Nothing succeeds like success. Success on one goal enhances the chance of success on subsequent goals.

2. Setting a goal which is too difficult or unrealistic is to set someone up to fail.

Using social learning theory as a basis for intervention, progress toward goals will be jointly reviewed by workers and clients, with a view to positive achievements, however small, being reinforced by the worker and new and appropriate goals being set.

Having set down the basics of a social learning theory approach to crisis intervention, let us now, by way of conclusion, summarise, and weave together, the various strands of the positive use of crisis outlined in this chapter.

Crisis, by its very nature, was seen to raise considerable potential for positive change. In a sense, a crisis reshuffles the pack, and thus, with a mixture of careful handling and good luck, a much better hand can be dealt.

Crisis is potentially both very destructive and very constructive. It can seriously undermine, on a long-term basis, one's 'level of functioning' in terms of coping mechanisms or it can lead to a much higher and more rewarding level of coping by exploiting the excellent learning opportunities afforded by the breakdown of homeostatic equilibrium. The crisis counsellor can be a major figure in determining which way the situation goes. The aim therefore is not simply to minimise the harm of a crisis, to 'cut losses', but rather to maximise the positive potential of crisis.

By examining the biological basis of the feelings experienced in crisis, it was seen that there is little or no difference in the physical sensations of extreme joy or extreme fear or anxiety. Thus, with some degree of training and positive support, as in assertiveness training, this physical 'buzz' can be used as a source of energy and motivation rather than inhibition and disincentive. Again, the role of the crisis counsellor can be crucial in positively harnessing this nervous energy. In doing so, weakness is turned into strength, and considerable potential harm becomes a very powerful source of positive and constructive energy.

Social learning theory was explored as a useful adjunct to crisis theory and the applicability and suitability of social learning principles to people in crisis were considered. The theory argues that the process of how we learn from our environment hinges on the key concept of reinforcement. If behaviour is positively reinforced, it is likely to be repeated. Reinforcement is particularly effective when it is sufficient, immediate and consistent (when establishing a new behaviour) or intermittent (when maintaining an existing behaviour). The theory is premised on the value of concentrating on the positive, and steadily building up an increased level of coping skills and confidence. This is facilitated by the key process of short-term, incremental goal-setting.

The two theoretical perspectives, crisis intervention and social learning theory, are highly compatible in that they both place great emphasis on making a virtue of concentrating on the positive and using it as both a tool and a principle of therapeutic intervention.

However, this compatibility should not be surprising, as one of the points to be made more fully in Chapter 4 is that one of the clear strengths of crisis intervention as a therapeutic method is that it does not preclude the use of other approaches. It offers great flexibility in terms of the repertoire of methods used within the crisis intervention framework.

The focus within this chapter on the positive dimension of crisis provides a very suitable backdrop for an examination of the practice of crisis intervention. We are therefore now ready to proceed to a consideration of 'doing crisis work'.

The next chapter focuses on issues relating to assessing crisis situations and this sets the scene for Chapter 4 which tackles the central issues of practising crisis intervention, the 'nuts and bolts' of practice.

Chapter 3

Assessment

Making an assessment of a situation in which people are hurt, angry, distressed or grieving is always difficult. It is not possible to apply straightforward, objective or 'scientific' criteria or methodology. A rigid approach is not only unlikely to succeed but may actually make the situation much worse by alienating or further distressing the client(s).

This much is true of all assessment but is particularly the case in crisis work. In crisis, clients are especially vulnerable and therefore good assessment work is vital to ensure that help is maximised and harm minimised.

But what are the principles of assessment which apply particularly to crisis intervention? An exploration of these principles, the skills required and the pitfalls to avoid, is precisely what we shall now undertake.

Principles of Crisis Assessment

1. Early assessment is crucial.

As crises are time-limited, it is extremely important to ensure that the assessment process is begun early. The exit phase of the crisis is when new solutions are found and of course it is at this point that unhelpful or counterproductive solutions can be adopted. It is therefore of major importance that an assessment and plan of intervention have been developed before the client(s) get too far into the exit phase. Delaying assessment is likely to result in 'missing the boat' and so the luxury of "well, let's see how it goes" cannot be afforded in crisis work.

2. Both the subjective and the objective dimensions must be included.

It is not only the 'objective', external circumstances which contribute to a crisis situation but also the subjective issues of emotional response, perception and interpretation. The assessment task is therefore twofold. On the one hand, the worker needs to know what has happened, what actions or events have played a part in producing a state of disequilibrium. On the other hand (and this is perhaps the more difficult task), the worker also needs to understand, as far as possible, the subjective issues, for example, the coping methods previously used, the emotional impact and overall personal significance of what has happened, the attitude towards future development and direction etc.

The relevant technical term is 'the precipitant', as we need to know not only the precipitant event, i.e. the objective 'trigger(s)' but also the personal psychological response which identifies the situation as a crisis. The concept of 'precipitant' therefore encompasses both objective and subjective dimensions, as a useful assessment must take account of both of these aspects.

3. Assessment should not have a narrow, psychological focus.

The traditional approach to crisis intervention is, as we saw in Chapter 1, a rather narrow one which focuses on psychological coping strengths. Wider social issues are mentioned but are not developed or fully integrated into the approach. In order to overcome this traditional weakness, good assessment must take account of two sets of wider, social factors:-

a) *Social resources for coping.* Family, friends, neighbours, welfare organisations, self-help groups etc. must be seen as part of the coping formula.

b) *Social location.* Social divisions such as class, race and gender are also significant parts of the coping formula. One's location in society can be plotted along these axes, and this social location (Berger 1963) will give important clues as to the pressures faced by the client(s) - e.g. economic pressures, racism, sexism etc. - and also potential sources of support - e.g. trade unions, black organisations, women's groups etc.

There is, however, a conflict here in terms of shortage of time in opposition to breadth of factors to be considered. It therefore needs to be recognised that pragmatic considerations of time will limit the breadth of the assessment. However, this should not be used as an excuse for concentrating only on the traditional, psychological factors. Crisis intervention is a psycho-social approach and so assessment should encompass both psychological and sociological issues.

31

4. Focus on the positive.

An assessment should not simply be a list of problems, worries or weaknesses. It is also necessary to identify areas of strength as the plan of intervention will seek to draw attention to these areas and build on them as a key part of the therapeutic process.

Identifying areas in which the client is coping well is significant for a number of reasons:-

a) It gives a baseline from which to build new coping methods in addition.

b) It helps to give client and worker a degree of confidence.

c) It gives opportunities for the worker to reinforce those coping skills (see Chapter 2) and immediately begin work on constructing a positive attitude and frame of reference.

Identifying strengths can be a difficult task for those workers who are schooled and experienced in more traditional problem-solving approaches in which the focus is clearly on an analysis of the negative elements with little reference to the positives.

Identifying and reinforcing strong points needs to be handled carefully and sensitively as it may give an impression that the worker is uninterested in the problems and has an unrealistically rosy picture of the situation. We shall return to this point below under the heading of 'skills required'.

5. Medicalisation should be avoided.

The temptation to simplify a complex psycho-social situation by applying a medical label is a temptation to be strongly resisted.

In crisis, a person's behaviour may be bizarre, unpredictable or self-destructive; sometimes behaviour may appear quite 'insane'. However, such behaviour must be seen in context, the context of a crisis in which usual coping mechanisms have broken down and left the person concerned feeling helpless and at a loss. We should be careful not to confuse such stress responses with mental illness. Such medicalisation (or 'psychiatrisation') merely distorts a complex and painful reality with social and psychological dimensions into a physiologically-based disease process. As Butcher and Maudal put it:-

"Formal psychiatric diagnosis is not particularly helpful in crisis therapy and may in fact be detrimental, in that it may orient the therapist toward seeing and planning for chronic pathology and blind him to important and manageable critical events." (1976, p618, quoted in Ewing, 1978, pp71-72)

Reliance on a medical diagnosis is therefore the easy way out, but, as we know, the easy way out is rarely the best way out and is often counterproductive in the long run.

Morrice (1976) also warns of the dangers of translating a crisis situation into a medical problem:-

"Distress should not be equated with psychiatric disorder although, of course, the latter may supervene if the situation becomes overwhelming." (p12)

In formulating an assessment, strange behaviour, e.g. a recently bereaved widow acting as if her husband is still with her, should be interpreted as a crisis response rather than the symptom of a mental illness. It is important to note that her acting in this way would be seen, from a crisis theory point of view, as a means of coping with her loss, a process of grieving and therefore a solution rather than a problem. We should be careful not to try to take away this coping method until she is ready to take on a better or more effective way of coping. In other words, we should not take away her crutch until she has been helped sufficiently to walk without its assistance. Assessment should take account of such issues.

6. The problem focus needs to be delineated (Ewing, 1978).

Clients in crisis are often not in a position to articulate their problems and so some degree of 'detective work', in the form of careful and sensitive questioning, is usually needed to clarify the focus of the problem. For example, the client may blame the 'last straw', the final event or action which ultimately provoked the crisis, whereas other factors, subjective and/or objective, may have been just as significant, if not more so. A person in crisis is likely to be confused and distraught and therefore not the best judge of the situation.

However, we need to be careful here and strike a balance. Crisis workers need to avoid taking over, invading their clients' territories and imposing their own definition of the situation. Where the views of worker and client differ, this must be discussed and as much agreement as possible reached. The reason for this is that crisis intervention is geared towards self-direction and empowerment. It is not possible to empower someone to follow a plan of action with which he/she disagrees. Only coercion, manipulation or persuasion can do this and none of these amounts to empowerment. (However, for an interesting discussion on the ethics of manipulation, see O'Hagan, 1986, Chapter 8.)

7. Clear plans need to be formulated.

The basic aim of assessment is to accumulate sufficient and appropriate information to produce a workable plan of intervention - i.e. an outline of what needs to be done and how it can/should be done.

Crisis is a time characterised by confusion, lack of structure and lack of control. In view of this scenario, it is therefore important that plans should be clear and easily understood. They should not be vague and woolly or ambiguous. Sharing such plans with a person in crisis will only add to the sense of being out of control and thus raise barriers to positive intervention. Clear, well-formulated, explicit plans can, on the contrary, help to re-establish control, order and meaning and thus prevent panic and deterioration. Sharing clear plans with a person in crisis therefore facilitates positive intervention and gets the whole process off to a beneficial and constructive start.

However, we should be careful not to confuse *clear* plans with *rigid* plans. In a crisis there are many unpredictable variables, and therefore plans need to be flexible and subject to easy review. There is a major difference between being clear about what you intend to do and being dogged or rigid about it. The former may include a willingness to change plans as and when circumstances dictate, whereas the latter certainly does not.

These, then, are what I see as the fundamental principles of crisis assessment, although I am by no means arguing that this is an exhaustive list. It is recognised that there are many other areas of assessment which could usefully be explored, but it is beyond the scope of this work to take the matter any further. It is to be hoped that I have at least provided a starting point from which people can launch themselves into developing good crisis assessment.

These principles as outlined are of course an important part of the process of assessment, but they are clearly not the only part. A second part, and one which has received relatively little attention, is that of skills development. Assessment in general is a skill-based activity, but crisis assessment needs to be especially skilful and relies on a particular set of skills. It is to an examination of such issues that we now turn.

Crisis Assessment Skills

1. Listening skills

The ability to listen effectively is a much valued one in social work and related areas of work, and not just in crisis work. However, successful crisis intervention has to be based on effective listening and yet the characteristics of a crisis situation - panic, high levels of emotion, possible physical danger, for example - can act as significant barriers to listening. Hearing what the client is trying to say can be prevented or obstructed in a number of ways, for example:-

a) Anxiety or fear on the worker's part can get in the way. The worker's own personal agenda may overrule the client's agenda. This may particularly be the case, where power and/or conflict are significant issues e.g. where a social worker is dealing with a case of child abuse and is considering removing the child(ren).

b) The interference of others who are also responding to the crisis, e.g. friends, relatives or people from other agencies, may make it difficult for the crisis counsellor to get the time and space to listen well. The good intentions and/or panic of others may therefore make the task of listening all the more difficult. However, it is also important to listen to what they have to say, as they too are part of the 'crisis matrix', the wider crisis situation.

c) Preconceptions can also be a hindrance. For example, when dealing with someone diagnosed as mentally ill, the worker may interpret valid thoughts, feelings and comments as 'symptomatic' of mental disorder (see principle no 5 above). Similarly, sexist or racist stereotypes may prevent workers from hearing what is actually being said.

One of the key skills of listening, therefore, is to remove as many barriers to communication as possible and thereby ensure that an appropriate atmosphere is created. In short, the worker needs to be able to make the time and space needed to listen. A major part of listening is allowing the client(s) to talk by doing whatever is possible to make this easy for them.

Furthermore, it should be remembered that 'listening' can also be used metaphorically to refer to taking on board non-verbal forms of communication (Hinde, 1972). Posture, gesture, touch etc., are significant dimensions of communication and, as we know (Argyle, 1972) verbal and non-verbal communications can contradict each other. It is necessary for crisis workers to 'listen' to both verbal and non-verbal messages and be sensitive to the extent to which they reinforce or contradict each other.

2. Reflecting feelings

By using reflection in a simple, non-judgmental and unbiased way, the helper conveys to those in crisis that he/she is trying to understand how they feel. Good reflection involves sensing not only what the client says but also how he/she says it.

By 'checking back' with the client in this way, the crisis worker achieves a number of things:-

a) Concern for the client is expressed, and this is both therapeutic in general terms and helps to 'lubricate' the interactions of the assessment process.

b) It limits opportunities for misunderstanding. If a worker reflects a feeling inaccurately or inappropriately, the misunderstanding is exposed and can be rectified. As the crisis assessment process needs to be a speedy one, built-in mechanisms for correcting misunderstandings are particularly valuable.

c) It humanises what can, at its worst, be a matter-of-fact process of gathering information. It begins the process of 'engaging' the client(s) and thus prepares the ground for the intervention stage proper.

Successful reflection of feelings is a delicate and sensitive skill which needs to be nurtured and developed.

An example of this skill in practice would be where, in response to a remark made in a tone of voice which suggests anger, the counsellor makes a comment along the lines of:-

> *"You seem to be quite angry. Do you want to talk about what's bothering you?"*

This type of response both shows empathy with the client and feeds back important information. For example, the client may not have realised he/she was expressing anger, as is often the case when emotions 'creep in' to our communications without our fully realising.

Of course, we should also not forget the reflection of feelings non-verbally. The crisis counsellor needs to be able to reflect feelings not only through words but also facial expressions, posture, physical distance, touch etc. Touch can be particularly effective but a note of caution is called for. Touch is a form of communication and so can easily be misinterpreted. We therefore need to be very clear about the message touch is conveying and that this is supported or confirmed verbally. Touch can be either very supportive or an oppressive invasion of personal space. If construed as the latter, a lot of harm can be done. Where the issue arises between a male worker and a female client, the question of sexual harassment can arise. This is a very real issue and a great cause for concern; it should not be dismissed or trivialised. I would therefore counsel caution by advising that touch be used selectively and sensitively.

3. Reinforcing coping skills

As was emphasised in Chapter 2, reinforcement of positives is a key aspect of crisis intervention. It forms a significant part of the intervention stage proper (see Chapter 4), but is also a fundamental component of the assessment process.

For a counsellor dealing with a client who is experiencing a crisis, one of the primary aims is to facilitate the learning of new techniques in coping. In order for the client to learn these skills, it is helpful for current skills, however minimal these may be in some cases, to be reinforced. For example, a new client expresses the following problem:-

> *"Meeting people and making conversation with them is very difficult for me."*

The counsellor's response may well be:-

> *"If that is so, then I think you have done really well to come here today and talk so openly about your feelings."*

With imagination, thought and practice, the skill of recognising opportunities to give positive reinforcement can be developed and put to very effective use.

Even in the most extreme of crisis situations it is likely that some areas of coping remain relatively unaffected and can be capitalised upon. Recognising these, and thus reinforcing them, is an assessment task.

In carrying out an assessment of a crisis situation, reinforcing coping skills can be helpful in the following ways:-

a) It identifies the client's strengths.

b) It gives an indication of how responsive he/she is to a positive approach.

c) It may reveal other significant aspects of the crisis matrix.

d) It helps to 'engage' the client and thus bridge the gap between the assessment stage and the intervention stage (although it should be noted that the two can never be entirely separated anyway as each implies elements of the other).

e) It encourages the client to share feelings and information.

Reinforcing coping skills is therefore part and parcel of assessment, but is itself a skill which needs to be developed. It requires the ability to:-

a) recognise positives even in an overwhelmingly negative situation;

b) reinforce these positives in a non-patronising and non-trivial way;

c) persuade the client to accept positives in a situation which is characterised by so many negatives.

As one might expect, developing this sort of skill is not easy but is nonetheless an important part of crisis assessment.

4. Non-provocative information gathering

In order to formulate a plan of intervention, it is necessary to obtain relevant and accurate information. As people in crisis are vulnerable and relatively powerless (and the worker very powerful) breaches of civil liberties can easily occur through over-intrusiveness. In view of this, the guiding principle of information-gathering should be to obtain the minimum information necessary rather than the maximum information available. Having said this, it is recognised that knowing what is the minimum, i.e. where to stop, is not as easy as it may sound. It has to be based on skill, experience and judgment. Relying on traditional casework notions of gathering as much information as possible is not appropriate to crisis intervention.

In addition to the civil liberties aspect, excessive probing or an overzealous seeking of information slows down what needs to be quite a rapid process and also it risks alienating the client(s). Information-gathering should therefore be non-provocative, and the skills necessary to ensure this should be practised and developed. Below I offer some guidelines as to how to move towards achieving this:-

a) Much information can be gained indirectly by 'ventilation'. That is, by creating for clients the right atmosphere to express their feelings, many relevant facts about the situation will emerge spontaneously without the need for direct questioning.

b) Crisis is a time when people are more open to any help offered and more likely to ask for help (Ewing, 1978, p13). It is therefore possible to elicit information about both the subjective and objective dimensions in a non-provocative, non-probing way simply by explaining what you need to know in order to be able to help. The information then needs to be clearly linked to the plan of action. This simple technique is important because it:-

   i) Focuses information and interaction. In a pressurised crisis situation, unfocused assessment is counter-productive.

   ii) It gives opportunities for positive reinforcement as it links information/assessment to strategy/intervention.

   iii) By explaining what information is needed and why, the worker confirms that the process is a shared one in which the client

39

plays an active part rather than a mysterious process in which the worker takes away the information and comes back with 'the answer'.

c) As was emphasised in Chapter 1, the traditional focus of crisis intervention is the individual. If we widen our focus to take in 'significant others' who are part of the crisis matrix, the necessary information can be gathered from a variety of sources and thus takes some of the pressure of 'probing' off the main characters in the crisis drama.

5. Calming and being calm

Crisis produces considerable emotion and nervous energy which often spills over into panic, aggression or even violence. A certain amount of giving vent to anger is of course helpful and constructive, but beyond a certain point and it becomes counter-productive and a barrier to progress.

Given that a crisis usually involves more than one person, too much tension and conflict can heighten ill-feeling and thus stand in the way of developing a positive and constructive approach. Some degree of control is therefore needed. The crisis worker needs to provide this control in three ways:-

a) To be able to calm the individual(s) concerned and help them to relax. Various techniques are available. (See Looker and Gregson, 1989)

b) To be able to mediate competently and successfully between people in conflict. Sometimes such conflict is the cause of the crisis (e.g. marital violence); sometimes it is the result of the crisis (e.g. the discovery that a child has been arrested for theft). Whichever applies, the crisis counsellor nonetheless has to be able to manage the situation sufficiently well to allow progress to be made.

c) To be able to manage one's own feelings for, as we shall see below, one of the dangers of crisis work is that it plunges the worker into a crisis of his/her own. It is therefore necessary to develop the skills required to deal with one's own emotional situation. As O'Hagan (1986) comments:-

"Social workers have a responsibility themselves to seek out their own potential fear, prejudice, panic, cowardice, stupidity, immorality and consequential incompetence in crisis situations. Discovering, recognising and acknowledging these dangerous vulnerabilities are the first and major step in minimising and controlling them." (p74)

The skills of calming and remaining calm are therefore vitally important for doing effective crisis work. This is particularly the case in the assessment stage, partly because the crisis participants are usually still in the early stages of crisis and are therefore particularly vulnerable, and partly because clear intervention plans cannot be formulated unless some degree of control over the situation has been achieved.

6. Time-management skills

One of the basic tenets of crisis intervention as a therapeutic method is that intensive short-term work is far more effective than less intensive work over a longer period (see Chapter 4 below).

What this means in effect is that the crisis worker is expected to devote a large amount of time to each case, as this is cost-effective in the long-run. This being the case, time-management becomes a very significant issue, especially for those people who work in settings where new crisis work must compete for priority with existing long-term non-crisis work.

Developing an effective and flexible time-management system and the skills required to operate it optimally is therefore a key part of the crisis worker's repertoire. Having such a flexible system is, after all, a coping mechanism and, as such, it helps the worker to maintain homeostasis and thus reduce the risk of a personal crisis on the worker's part.

To carry out a good assessment of a crisis situation involves being in the right place at the right time; therefore considerable flexibility is needed. However, those who opt for total flexibility, at the expense of a system, run the risk of losing control of their workload and losing track of priorities. The fact that someone is in crisis does not automatically mean that he or she is a priority compared with other work tasks. The priorities need to be assessed in the context of the knowledge that crisis theory gives us of the therapeutic potential of crisis, but this should not blind us to the need to appreciate competing priorities. For example, rushing out to deal with a minor crisis may mean we are not available when a much more serious crisis arises. Technology can be of assistance here in terms of radio-pagers, mobile phones etc., but these cannot be a substitute for a system of managing one's time to maximum effect.

Acquiring time-management skills is by no means an easy task, but the efforts required should be repaid, with dividends, by the rewards of such a set of useful skills.

7. Self-care skills

This is probably the most important set of skills of all. Crisis work can be very stressful, demanding, challenging and potentially harmful to one's health and wellbeing. Many workers find crisis intervention exciting, exhilarating and very rewarding, but this can very easily turn sour in a number of ways. This is again particularly the case in the very demanding assessment stage where no clear plan of work has emerged, where feelings are running high and where the people involved are unknown to the worker. In view of this potential danger, there is a clear need for a strong emphasis on self care. This is important for two reasons - first, for the obvious personal benefit of the worker and, second, for the benefit of clients; a crisis worker on sick leave due to nervous exhaustion is not much use to his/her clients. Cutting corners on self-care is therefore a false economy.

In Chapter 7, I shall address issues of staff care, the responsibilities I feel employers have for safeguarding and supporting their staff. What I wish to emphasise here, however, is self-care, the part played by employees rather than employers. The two sets of issues, self-care and staff-care, should of course interlock but the absence of one should not be allowed to hinder the development of the other. Both elements are important, if not crucial.

Skill development can be directed towards the following areas:-

a) *Time-out.* Despite the demands of crisis, time must be found for 'time-out'. This should be in the form of regular breaks, extra hours worked being taken as 'time off in lieu', time to think, relax and discuss. (This should be part of the time-management system referred to above.) A worker who gets caught up in the hectic pace

42

of a crisis needs to slow the pace as far as possible and actually manage the situation - and this should include allowing space for time-out. Crisis workers who contribute to their own premature burn-out are not doing their clients, their employers or themselves any favours.

b) *Protection.* Crisis situations are often potential sources of violence; in many cases the worker may become involved either coincidentally, by being in the wrong place at the wrong time, or as a direct result of his/her role, e.g. the compulsory hospitalisation of a mentally disordered person or the removal of a child to a place of safety. Where such potential violence is anticipated, the worker should insist on having a colleague present, or even a police officer if the risk is significantly high.

Other techniques for preventing/avoiding violence (sometimes referred to as 'conflict management') can also be drawn on. Developing the appropriate skills is therefore to be encouraged.

c) *Drawing the line.* When crisis work gets the adrenalin flowing, it may become difficult to 'switch off' and draw the line between work and home life. There is a little point having the discipline to take much needed breaks during work time, if one's personal and social life are dominated by work issues or anxieties. 'Drawing the line' is therefore vital, as trying to cope with other people's crises 24 hours a day is a certain recipe for disaster - the perennial danger: crisis work produces a crisis in the worker. Methods of relaxing and switching off from work should therefore be actively sought.

This is of course not an exhaustive list but will hopefully suffice to emphasise the point that neglecting the development of self-care skills is a risky business and is not only potentially disastrous but actually positively courts disaster.

The seven skill areas outlined here are basic building bricks of good assessment work and, as we have emphasised, good assessment is particularly important in crisis work as the timescale of the whole operation is so telescoped.

Most, if not all, of these skills will be needed for, and relevant to, the intervention stage proper as assessment and intervention tend to merge anyway. The distinction between the two stages is of course more a matter of emphasis than a hard and fast boundary. But, before moving on to consider strategies of intervention, let us first round off our examination of assessment by outlining some common pitfalls which require careful navigation if they are to be avoided.

Pitfalls to be Avoided

1. Crisis begets crisis

This is perhaps something of a leitmotif in this work but I feel it is sufficiently important to merit such emphasis. It is in fact two pitfalls in one. On the one hand, it means that the worker's own coping resources need to be strong and extensive to prevent the situation also being a trigger for a crisis in the worker (insofar as existing coping mechanisms break down and homeostasis is destroyed). On the other hand, it means that where a crisis does occur on the worker's part, this needs to be recognised and dealt with accordingly. What we have learned from crisis theory applies not only to clients in crisis but also to workers.

The twofold pitfall to avoid therefore is:

a) plunging into crisis oneself and

b) where this does occur, failing to recognise the fact and therefore not seeking the appropriate help.
(As we shall see in Chapter 7, crisis work should not be a solitary activity.)

2. Moving not at the client's pace

In the heat of crisis, it is a mistake all too easily made to press on as fast as possible, given the time constraints crisis intervention imposes, but thereby move too fast for the client(s). In crisis situations time is of the essence, but this is no excuse for not moving at the client's pace. It may well be necessary to speed up the client's pace at times, for example through encouragement, but it is nonetheless important to adhere to that pace.

Crisis intervention is geared towards empowering people in crisis to draw on the positive potential and thereby increase their coping resources and capabilities. This cannot be done except at the client's pace.

3. Seeing a crisis that is not there

Some situations are characterised by high drama and intense emotional impact but are not, in fact, crises. A crisis is the breakdown of routine coping methods, a discontinuity in homeostasis. Such dramatic incidents, e.g. a heated argument in which violence is threatened, may be unusual and suggestive of crisis to most people, but for some may be a routine way for coping and thus not a crisis at all. It would therefore be inappropriate to apply crisis intervention principles in such circumstances.

It should be remembered that crisis is both a subjective and an objective phenomenon. No matter how dramatic or 'crisis-like' the objective circumstances may seem, if the subjective perceptions of the people involved do not see it as a crisis, it is not a crisis.

An inexperienced worker, dealing with a couple who yell at each other at the top of their voices, may not feel able to handle the situation but, if this is the case, his/her crisis as a worker should not be confused with a crisis on the couple's part.

The pitfall to be avoided, therefore, is that of seeing a crisis where none exists.

4. Seeking consensus

As O'Hagan (1986) points out, one of the basic characteristics of crisis is its conflictual nature, although this is something the 'pioneers' did not address. He comments:-

> "What Caplan and his colleagues in those flower-power, liberating sixties did not realise was something that no social worker could fail to notice: crises are primarily about conflict - conflict between one individual and another, individual and family, individual and agency. It could be a conflict of interests, perceptions, loyalties, values or emotions, and any of these is capable of erupting in actual physical conflict." (p29)

If we accept that conflict is part and parcel of crisis, surely arriving at consensus is a short path to crisis resolution? This, however is a problematic position to adopt, partly because it is somewhat naive (is consensus feasible or is it idealistic?) and partly because it would amount to 'crisis survival' (see Chapter 1) rather than crisis intervention.

Whilst O'Hagan is right to argue that conflict characterises crisis, we should note that conflict can also be seen as a characteristic of human existence, especially within the framework of existentialist philosophy, as discussed in Chapter 1. (See Sartre, 1976. This is particularly the case when that existence is characterised by such oppressive social divisions as class, race, gender, etc.). This being the case, the crisis intervention task should not simply be to attempt to resolve the immediate conflict (although this may be a key part of the overall strategy) but rather to empower the crisis participants to manage conflict more effectively and successfully.

The pitfall here, therefore, is to pursue a chimerical goal of consensus, whereas it should be one of gaining the strength and skills to handle conflict as and when it arises.

5. Seeking certainty

There are few certainties in life. Some thinkers, such as Sartre, even go so far as to say that only one's eventual death is certain. However, in parallel fashion to pitfall no 4 above, we often seek a chimerical goal of certainty when some hint of probability may be the most that can be afforded.

The casework tradition of assessment is based on a 'diagnosis' phase which entails planning on the basis of as much relevant information as possible. As we have already seen, this approach is not appropriate to crisis intervention due to the urgency involved. However, the strength of the traditional approach is that the degree of certainty/ probability, upon which one bases one's intervention, is maximised. Crisis workers have to operate on much lower margins of probability. Seeking certainty, or even a high degree of probability before one acts is likely to amount to paralysis. The pace of crisis dictates a much less cautious approach (although this is no excuse for throwing all caution to the wind), otherwise there may be a hiatus between the assessment and intervention phases, and this is likely to result in 'missing the boat' as new and perhaps inappropriate coping mechanisms are adopted while the worker is still making up his/her mind what to do. This pitfall therefore, is allowing one's intolerance of uncertainty to produce inaction or delay necessary action.

These, then, are just a few of the many pitfalls to be encountered in the minefield of crisis intervention in general and the assessment stage in particular. In combination with an understanding of the principles of crisis counselling and the associated skills, an awareness of these pitfalls will hopefully help to equip workers to undertake good quality assessment of crisis situations and thus build a clear plan of intervention.

Having set the scene for a discussion of the actual process of intervention, let us now bring our analysis of assessment issues to a close and thereby move on to explore the how, where, when, what and why of crisis intervention.

Chapter 4

Intervention

Crisis theory may well be a valuable guide to understanding what happens in crises and the way in which a crisis affects people. But how, you may be asking, can this be used in a pragmatic way to guide social workers dealing with people in crisis? Chapter 3 has shown us how the insights can be used to assess the situation, but this is a long way from actually doing something about resolving the situation. So, to put it technically, how can crisis theory be operationalised, how can it 'pay its dues' by being of clear, positive and direct help to crisis workers?

In order to try to answer these questions, this chapter will follow the same basic pattern as Chapter 3. I shall first of all spell out what I see as the basic principles of crisis intervention, followed by a discussion of the skills workers need to develop in order to use these principles as an effective guide to practice. Finally, I shall examine some of the pitfalls to be avoided, some of the mistakes that can easily be made in the fraught atmosphere of crisis.

It needs to be recognised that, although I am aiming to bridge theory and practice, I cannot provide a simple formula for workers to follow. I can, however, provide a framework which is not simply 'interesting' but can be of practical value in helping people cope positively with crises.

I shall begin with the principles which govern crisis intervention.

Principles of Crisis Intervention

These principles are based on a wide range of sources, including my own practice experience, but in particular I should acknowledge reference to Ewing (1978) and Morrice (1976).

1. Delay in intervention tends to be costly.

The sooner intervention begins, the better. During the impact and recoil stages of crisis, there is little that can be done by way of counselling, as the participants tend to be emotionally numbed and thus unresponsive. However, being involved in the early stages has three advantages, as follows:-

a) Early assessment can begin.

b) Simply 'being there' helps to engage the client(s) and thereby set the scene for positive intervention.

c) Appropriate resources (support networks, etc.) can be mobilised or identified ready for mobilisation at the appropriate time.

When a crisis situation is encountered, considerable nervous energy is generated (Parkes, 1987, Ch 3) and this sudden thrust of energy can be a source of strong motivation and determination. This is a major resource which both clients and worker can draw upon as part of the problem-solving process. Previous routine patterns of behaviour are abandoned and new ways of coping are sought. This is a very fruitful time for intervention to take place, as the nervous energy characteristic of crisis can be harnessed positively and used constructively to try to make whatever changes are necessary to resolve the crisis.

At such a highly charged, volatile and threatening time, it is very tempting indeed to use 'crisis survival' techniques, for example by waiting for things to 'cool down' by staying off the scene for a while. The net result of such a strategy is likely to be to 'miss the boat' by failing to capitalise on the change resources produced by the crisis.

If intervention is delayed, the client(s) may have resolved the crisis in some other way and may thus produce a solution which is not going to be helpful when future stresses and potential crises are brewing. For example, a woman who becomes disabled may give up her job because, still in crisis, she cannot cope with the pressures. The loss of job, income, status, social contacts, etc., thus makes her more vulnerable to crisis. The short-term gain (crisis survival) is a long-term loss. Early intervention could perhaps have helped her cope with the job in the interim, or arrange 'time-out', thus seeking a more positive outcome of the crisis.

The fact that crisis intervention requires early involvement has serious implications for the organisational structure in which the crisis worker operates; a system which takes two weeks or more to allocate referrals more or less kills the opportunity for maximal crisis intervention. This is a point to which I shall return in Chapter 7.

2. Intensive short-term work is more effective than extensive long-term work.

This is related to the first principle, namely the value of early intervention. Putting in a great deal of effort to produce constructive change pays dividends in the long run as the crisis produces the energy and motivation to develop stronger and more effective methods of coping which will:

> a) help to prevent future crises,
>
> b) improve confidence and self-esteem, and
>
> c) contribute to a better quality of life.

Because clients tend to be more receptive to help when they are in crisis, considerable movement towards desired goals can be achieved in a relatively short period of time, carried by the vehicle of the motivation generated by the crisis. The 'fight or flight' mechanism, if channelled positively can direct the client's actions towards effective problem-solving and thus build up coping resources.

These resources are, as I stressed earlier, not simply psychological ones but also include wider familial, community, social and institutional ones. The response of significant individuals, groups or agencies will often be stronger and more supportive in times of crisis than at times of routine requests for assistance. The energy and drama of the crisis can therefore 'suck in' external coping resources in ways which do not apply to non-crisis situations. For example, housing departments may well be more sympathetic to a family's housing problems when a crisis situation obtains than is usually the case.

In long-term social work much time, effort and energy are expended in seeking to motivate clients towards constructive change. This is so often an uphill struggle; clients quite understandably tend to offer much resistance as the situation implies an externally defined change i.e. change on the social worker's terms rather than the client's. This is very problematic, as this comment from Marris illustrates:-

> "To be told the meaning of your life by others, in terms which are not yours, implies that your existence does not matter to them, except as it is reflected in their own." (1986, p155)

This is a major 'occupational hazard' for long-term social workers who may be geared more towards 'maintaining' a situation i.e. the focus is on preventing deterioration rather than bringing about improvement (Corby, 1982). Crisis workers are in a much more 'luxurious' position in terms of the positive potential for change. Realising that potential can thus obviate the need for later long-term work.

3. Listening is a key activity.

Crisis workers are in a powerful position in dealing with vulnerable, relatively helpless clients. It is therefore extremely important that the trouble is taken actually to listen to what clients are saying. As I shall stress below, providing the 'right answer' without listening to clients is of no help and potentially very harmful. Intervention needs to take account of both the objective dimension and the subjective dimension for, as we have seen, crisis operates at, and affects both dimensions. The latter dimension, that of the subjective area of perceptions, emotions and values, necessarily involves listening. To operate purely or mainly at the objective level - where the worker is relatively powerful - amounts merely to crisis survival as it does not equip the client(s) to cope any better with the next crisis. The subjective dimension is an intense area with potent emotional storms and a devastating sense of loss. Here, the worker feels powerless and can easily feel overwhelmed by the raw emotion. Because of this, listening can be painful, distressing and can itself provoke a crisis in the worker. Good practice in crisis intervention must nonetheless be premised on good and effective listening (and 'listening' can also be understood to refer, metaphorically, to being sensitive to non-verbal communication).

Listening is of course a key aspect of assessment and therefore plays an important part in the early stages, but the point I am making here is that it is vital to keep listening throughout the intervention process. In crisis, both feelings and circumstances can change rapidly and so the worker needs to remain 'tuned in' to the crisis scenario.

4. A repertoire of methods is available.

Crisis intervention is not a specific social work method which implies the exclusion of other methods. Rather, it is a theoretical framework which guides us in certain directions and provides certain insights, but which does not offer a simple formula for 'putting things right'.

One of the basic tenets of crisis theory is that human existence is complex, fraught, vulnerable and uncertain; hence the need for us to equip ourselves, both socially and psychologically, for the stress, trauma and crises implicit in such an existence. Given this model, a step by step prescription for practice would be both inadequate and inappropriate.

The framework of crisis intervention assumes that there is a wide repertoire of coping skills and resources which can be drawn upon through therapeutic endeavour. In parallel fashion, a repertoire of social work methods can be drawn upon to fulfil the goals identified by applying a crisis intervention framework. To put it technically, crisis intervention is a theoretical perspective rather than a method or technique.

At a theoretical/conceptual level, crisis intervention may be contradicted by other social work approaches. For example, crisis theory is premised on human freedom and responsibility for one's actions, whilst behaviourism, another social work favourite, eschews such notions as idealistic. However, at the level of practice, useful and effective behavioural techniques can be uprooted from their deterministic background and 'replanted' in the more humanistic context of crisis theory. This amounts not to using behaviourism instead of crisis intervention, but rather to using behavioural methods (e.g. reinforcement of positives) in a way which is consistent with, and therefore part of, a crisis intervention programme. [1]

The theoretical issues relating to the problem of using fundamentally incompatible approaches need not concern us here. Suffice to note that crisis intervention does not compete with other approaches or methods, but rather provides an overarching framework which helps to guide, and illuminate, our practice.

Behaviourism has been chosen as an example, but the same argument applies to family therapy, Rogerian counselling, transactional analysis or whatever other tool we choose to employ.

---

[1] However, note that reliance on behaviourist techniques alone is not enough; this needs to be counterbalanced by actions that also take account of the subjective dimension.

5. Intervention should be future-oriented.

Crisis involves a significant element of loss and especially loss of control; it is therefore not surprising that clients should concentrate on the past, either as part of a grieving process or as part of an attempt to make sense of what has led to the present confused and painful situation. This in itself is helpful, but it can easily take up excessive time and energy and prevent the client from moving on.

Where this situation becomes problematic, it is often described as 'crying over spilled milk'. As Morrice (1976) puts it, the focus should be on future planning, not on past mistakes.

A crisis generates considerable nervous energy and motivation and this needs to be focused on future actions, on how to cope better in respect of the next crisis and the one after that, and so on. Working out what mistakes were made previously may form a part of this, but it should be limited to a small part, as once again the emphasis should be on positive strengths as building self-confidence is a crucial part of developing new coping skills or exploring/cultivating new support systems.

Focusing on the future is also very significant in terms of generating hope - again a key element in crisis intervention - as hope is a reflection of our (positive) attitude to the future.

A crisis is a situation which has overpowered us, which appears to have minimised our control over our circumstances, over our lives. In these conditions we are literally 'alienated' - we feel that our lives are not our own. Reinstating this sense of ownership of our own lives is a fundamental part of instilling hope and bringing about post-crisis rebuilding.

Part of this future orientation is the need to avoid attributing blame. Whether this blame is directed inwards towards oneself as guilt or outwards towards others as censure, it has little or no therapeutic value and should therefore be discouraged.

To pinpoint who is or was to blame may possibly clarify who or what contributed to the crisis or it may cloud the issue. Regardless of this, from a therapeutic point of view, attributing blame is unhelpful as it prevents the client(s) from moving on.

Social workers should therefore discourage this and should most certainly avoid engaging in it themselves, although clients in crisis will often pressurise workers to do so in order to reinforce their own view of who is to blame.

6. Intervention should be time-limited.

One of the key characteristics of crisis as identified by the classical theory of crisis intervention is that of being 'time-limited'. Crises are relatively short-lived; we tend to 're-equilibrate' ourselves fairly quickly as homeostasis is far preferable to the trauma and anguish of crisis. Intervention should also reflect this by having a clear, but flexible time limit.

One of the dangers of working with people in crisis is that they can become dependent. The crisis worker can be viewed as a coping resource to be drawn upon when future crises loom and this can demotivate clients from developing their own coping skills or 'plugging in' to appropriate support systems. it is therefore important that the crisis worker does not stay involved any longer than is necessary and makes it clear that his/her involvement will only be temporary.

A useful strategy for achieving this is to state explicitly in the early stages of intervention that help will be offered only while needed i.e. on a short-term basis. This can be the basis of a contract, an agreed set of shared objectives to be pursued within a realistic timescale (realistic in terms of the predicted timescale of the crisis).

There are two major advantages to this strategy:-

i) It does not give clients false expectations about a prolonged period of intervention and support.

ii) It introduces a degree of control and stability into a situation characterised by absence of control and equilibrium.

Time-limited contract work is therefore a popular option for those workers who favour a crisis intervention approach. There are, however, two 'riders' which need to be added to this in order to avoid the potential drawbacks of this strategy. They are:-

i) Time targets must be flexible. It is pointless closing a case simply because the agreed timescale has expired. The case should only be closed when the agreed initial (or renegotiated) objectives have been met or accepted as unattainable. The discipline of a time-scale should therefore be seen as a means to an end rather than an end in itself.

ii) When a case is closed, clients are likely to need the reassurance that they are not debarred from future help if/when this is required. In other words it needs to be made clear that the closing of a case does not amount to 'closing the door' for good. Very often the security offered by knowing that a 'safety net' exists can give people the confidence to cope (We shall re-emphasise this again below).

Time-limited intervention should not therefore be used as an appropriate tool of workload management by closing cases prematurely.

7. Crisis intervention is proactive.

One of the common misunderstandings of crisis intervention is that it is reactive, i.e. it is not preventative. Of course, this is most certainly not the case; the primary aims of crisis intervention are to facilitate the learning of new and better coping skills and greater use of support networks. [1] These activities are clearly proactive insofar as they are geared towards preventing future crises.

However, what should also not be forgotten is that this does not limit us to waiting for crises to happen (or worse still, playing the potentially disastrous game of provoking crises) as the principles of crisis intervention can equally be applied on a much wider basis. For example, social workers can become involved in training people in coping skills, especially with regard to those people who may be more prone to crisis (such as mentally disordered people). Similarly, other forms of preventative social or community work, e.g. benefit take-up campaigns to help alleviate poverty, are consistent with crisis intervention.

In terms of prevention, crisis intervention gives us two messages:-

i) Any work which helps to prevent crises is to be encouraged. This includes reducing stress/distress on the one hand and boosting coping skills and support networks on the other.

---

(1) Note that this parallels the Barclay Report distinction between counselling and social care planning. (Barclay, 1982)

ii) Effective crisis intervention should teach people how to prevent future crises where possible and how to cope better with those that cannot be prevented.

These, then, are the major principles of crisis intervention, but of course many other such principles could be deduced if time and space permitted. Having outlined these practice principles, we now need to make them more concrete and more accessible by discussing the skills that I see as being necessary for putting such principles into practice, that is for converting crisis theory into crisis intervention. I shall follow the same pattern as for the previous chapter by outlining the relevant skills before moving on to discuss pitfalls to be avoided.

Crisis Intervention Skills

What needs to be made clear from the outset is that the skills already discussed in relation to crisis assessment will also be very relevant and valuable in the intervention phase proper. In particular, the ability to listen, to reflect feelings and to reinforce coping skills are key parts of effective intervention.

1. Risk analysis

Crisis necessarily involves risk for all concerned for, as we have seen, crisis is precisely a time when contingency is to the fore, when uncertainty and instability are very much in evidence.

This has three major implications for social workers:-

a) The degree of risk to clients, their families, associates, etc., needs to be carefully and thoroughly assessed. Child protection and approved social worker duties are examples of work where such risk analysis is crucial.

b) The risk faced by the worker also needs to be given due attention. Violence to social workers is not unheard of and the highly charged atmosphere of crisis may make such violence all the more possible. Social workers should therefore make every effort to safeguard themselves from harm, e.g. by doing certain visits accompanied. Being attacked by a client in crisis does the social worker no good, and the likely repercussions of such an attack will not do the client any favours either.

c) Taking informed and well thought-out risks is an essential part of crisis intervention and so the worker should be ready and willing to take appropriate risks as and when the circumstances dictate. Maximising the positive potential of a crisis necessarily involves some degree of gambling. A crisis worker who is not prepared to take risks or is ill-equipped to make informed judgments or risk is highly unlikely to be an effective crisis worker.

In sum, risk is integral to crisis intervention and it is therefore important for crisis workers to build up the skills of risk analysis: a sensitivity to the balance between over-caution on the one hand and reckless risk-taking on the other. Allied to this is the ability to cope with the intense contingency of the minefield of risks social workers face. Parton's (1985) discussion of the 'no-win scenario' of child abuse investigation underscores this point.

2. Patience

Patience may be a virtue but it is also a skill. It is related to the concept, introduced earlier, of working at the client's pace.

Crisis work can be very frustrating and can seriously try our patience. It is something of an 'occupational hazard' to have to resist strong feelings of moving the client quickly on when he or she is not yet ready to make progress. Conversely, a client may wish to hurtle on at breakneck speed whilst the worker feels a gentler pace is more prudent.

The worker's patience may be tested in a number of other ways:-

– important advice may be ignored or notes of caution unheeded;

– a key member of the support network may withdraw;

– co-operation from other professionals may be lacking or they may adopt a judgmental or oppressive standpoint (e.g. racist, sexist or ageist);

– the institutional resources needed may not be available.

The danger here is to fall into the essentialist trap of seeing patience as a quality which some people have but which others do not. Patience is a skill or a pattern of behaviour which can be learned or developed. As crisis intervention tends to make demands on one's patience, it pays dividends to develop this skill, or set of skills - controlled emotional expression, unconditional positive regard, the ability to think clearly and work effectively whilst under pressure. These all come under the umbrella of patience and are indispensable components of the crisis worker's repertoire. They are not inbred parts of one's personality, but rather skills/behaviour which can be learned and improved through practice, effort and discussion.

3. Confrontation

Diplomacy is clearly recognised as an important skill in social work in general and is of no less value in crisis intervention in particular. Tactlessness is certainly no advantage in crisis work. However, there are times when diplomacy needs to be counter-balanced by the appropriate and skilful use of confrontation.

As clients enter the exit phase of the crisis, they may adopt unhelpful, counterproductive or harmful methods of coping, such as excessive drinking or other forms of avoidance behaviour. In such circumstances, it will be the task of the crisis worker to effect a confrontation but without alienating the clients concerned. This involves a delicate and subtle balance, and thus a skilled approach is called for.

This is parallel with the notion of 'non-provocative probing' applied in the earlier assessment phase - the need to tackle delicate issues firmly but sensitively. As O'Hagan (1986) points out, crises are characterised by conflicts of various kinds and therefore effective crisis intervention entails being able and willing to confront such conflicts head on, thus helping clients to move on by resolving, or learning how to manage, the conflicts they encounter.

Skilful confrontation hinges on a number of factors:-

– the courage to tackle painful, anxiety-provoking or contentious issues;

– the ability to work calmly under such pressures (and also to instil calmness);

– self-awareness in recognising and dealing with one's own feelings and interests in relation to the conflictual situation;

– good communication. Care should be taken to ensure that confrontation is not interpreted as a personal attack or aggression.

Thus, there are two extremes to steer clear of - avoiding confrontation on the one hand (the 'safety first' approach) and using it overzealously on the other (the 'over-the-top' approach).

4. Motivation and self-motivation

Self-motivation is something which is seen in commonsense terms as a quality rather than a skill. However, crisis theory is an example of an approach which denies 'essentialism', the view that we are burdened or otherwise with fixed characteristics. Our patterns of behaviour and thought reflect our characteristic methods of coping and our skills, rather than a fixed essence. Consequently, we can learn to motivate ourselves; we can learn to seek satisfaction from the work we do. Hopefully, reading texts such as this is part of that process.

Crises produce considerable nervous energy and, as Chapter 2 illustrated, this can be used either positively or negatively. The energy is produced not only in the clients and their associates but also in the worker. Positive use of crisis entails using this energy to motivate oneself.

Crises are a minefield of several different emotions for all concerned. In carrying out crisis intervention, the social worker is prone to frustration, fear, anger, even depression and must be able not only to cope with these but also to instil positive feelings in clients and in himself/herself, i.e. to motivate and be motivated. There are a range of skills involved in this, primarily communication skills on the one hand (motivation), and self-awareness skills on the other (self-motivation). It is therefore an unacceptably easy way out to say "self-motivation is not one of my strong points". Being involved in crises means that our thoughts, feelings and patterns of behaviour are often 'on the line', and we are vulnerable to criticism and self-criticism. Crisis work is not a 'safe', comfortable or clinical approach to therapeutic work; this means that opportunities to learn about ourselves and build on what we learn are never very far away.

The need to build upon such learning is also everpresent. This is an exciting and challenging aspect of crisis work and is a key element in the art of self-motivation. Being self-motivated in itself goes some way towards motivating others as it sets a positive tone for the intervention. This can be supplemented by 'motivational counselling' and also by advocacy or other forms of helping to change the objective circumstances which may be demotivating. This is consistent with the principle that both the subjective and the objective dimensions of the situation must be taken into account.

5. Termination

I have already argued that intervention should be time-limited in order to prevent dependency. One of the major implications of this is that social workers, as they build up experience of crisis work, should seek to develop the skills of terminating intervention as effectively as possible.

It is not enough simply to announce that involvement is to cease. Hopefully, by this stage the client(s) will be much stronger and thus less vulnerable. Nonetheless a badly handled termination may undo much of the good which has previously been done. At this stage in the proceedings, a client's confidence is likely to be rather tentative and somewhat precarious. It is therefore unwise to risk this by withdrawing abruptly. This may provoke a further crisis.

One of the characteristics of crisis we have identified is the lack of control, the breakdown of homeostasis. Part of the crisis worker's task is to help bring the situation under control. The client may therefore come to associate control and stability with the worker and thus feel very threatened by his/her withdrawal from the scene. Termination therefore needs to be handled carefully and sensitively.

As with any other situation which needs to be managed carefully, there are three clear dimensions to this:-

– *Analysis*. The component parts of the situation need to be recognised and understood.

– *Planning*. A haphazard, 'take it as it comes' approach is unnecessarily risky. Termination is not just the end of intervention but rather a key part of that intervention. Planning therefore has an important role to play.

– *Control*. The social worker needs to take some degree of responsibility for the situation and ensure that it goes to plan, as far as is practicable.

This model is also applicable to the types of intervention where termination is likely to be welcomed by the clients involved. An example of this would be a child protection case that has been resolved. Although the situation may be such that the case can safely be closed, the feelings generated by the crisis may lead to bitterness and considerable ill-feeling or even emotional harm if termination is rushed or mishandled.

6. Applying Theory to Practice

Qualifying training courses have long stressed the value and importance of applying theory to practice. This is often a cause for concern amongst students as there is no clear, straightforward way of translating theory into practice, and yet the need to do so is constantly emphasised.

The same situation obtains in relation to crisis intervention. Crises are fraught, complex and demanding; it is therefore not possible simply to apply a formula or standardised approach. However, there still remains considerable value in drawing upon a professional knowledge base for, as we have warned, dealing with crises in a 'commonsense' way amounts to 'crisis survival', an ineffective and potentially harmful response to crisis.

In short, doing 'crisis intervention' without reference to crisis theory is, in effect, not crisis intervention, but rather this poor relation called 'crisis survival'.

There is a set of skills involved in applying theory to practice. Many social workers avoid developing these skills by adopting the anti-intellectual stance of claiming to prefer to 'stick to practice'. For those who take a less ostrich-like approach to the rather thorny issues of integrating theory and practice, the appropriate skills need to be developed. As a first step towards this, we can readily identify some of the skills which are particularly appropriate in putting crisis theory into action:-

– recognising the stages (impact/recoil/exit);

– identifying positives to build on;

– encompassing the subjective and objective dimensions;

– recognising both the psychological and the wider social aspects.

These are of course only a small selection from a wide range, but hopefully this will at least give a flavour of practice grounded in theory.

7. Anti-discriminatory practice

In recent years social work has started to pay serious attention to issues of oppression and discrimination on the grounds of class, race, gender, age, disability and sexual orientation. In many areas, explicit equal opportunities policies exist, at a rhetorical level at least, and social work education in particular has made strenuous efforts to take these issues on board.

There has therefore been progress at a policy level (although there is a long way to go yet), but to date little attention has been paid to the actual skills required to practise in an anti-discriminatory way.

There is a strong parallel here with the question of applying theory to practice. A body of knowledge is being developed (anti-discriminatory policy/theory/values), but there is then a quantum leap to the grassroots level of practice, with only a very vague and sketchy bridge between the two.

Addressing these issues satisfactorily is far beyond the scope of this text but, on a more realistic scale, we can consider some of the skills issues which arise in relation to anti-discriminatory crisis work.

One of the key skills must be developing a sensitivity to the impact of social divisions on clients' lives. For example, in a family crisis, gender roles and patriarchal social relations are likely to feature significantly. If, for example, that family were black, the oppression of racism would also merit being taken into account.

The other side of this is, of course, our own discrimination. In keeping with crisis theory, we need to consider both the objective dimension (the effects of discrimination on clients in terms of social pressures, coping skills and support networks), and the subjective (our own attitudes, values, assumptions which are brought to bear in our work). Anti-discriminatory practice entails recognising the impact of oppression on clients *and* how discriminatory ideologies (racism, sexism, ageism etc.) impinge upon and subtly influence our thoughts, feelings, attitudes and actions. After years of relative neglect, social work is now starting to address both sets of issues. Crisis intervention can be no exception to this. In the heat of crisis, social workers are pressurised yet powerful people; the potential for oppression and discrimination being unintentionally reproduced or reinforced presents a scenario which requires skilful handling.

Some of the skills outlined here are well-established and much in evidence in good practice across various social work agencies and settings. For other skills, however, there are fewer role models, fewer guidelines and less clarity. The challenge for crisis workers is therefore not simply to learn traditional skills, but also to forge new skills in building a crisis intervention which befits modern social work.

Pitfalls to be Avoided

1. False assumptions

These can be made by either client or worker - or both. Things happen fast in crisis and it is therefore not surprising that communication can be reduced and important factors overlooked. Thus it is a simple but costly mistake to jump to conclusions. The pressure to get things done and 'strike while the iron is hot' can lead to assumptions being made which, in less pressurised times, would have been checked out.

This applies equally to clients and workers. Workers can base their intervention on false assumptions or misinformation and therefore be off-target in terms of the plans carried out. For example, a social worker may send an important letter to a client, notifying him or her of an important issue, but then assume, perhaps wrongly, that the letter was received. Similarly a client may express an intention to discuss the situation with another significant party and, in the heat of crisis, the worker may assume that this has happened when in reality it may not have.

In parallel fashion, clients may base their actions on incorrect information or false assumptions. Hopefully this is something that will have been picked up at the assessment stage, but it can easily be missed and then emerge at a crucial point in the intervention process. For example, a child care crisis may arise as a result of marital conflict. This conflict may be founded on a misunderstanding (and we know how often conflicts are based on misunderstanding), for example the unfounded suspicion of infidelity. Tension over one issue, e.g. an accusation of child abuse, can easily spill over into other areas. Suspicion, mistrust and jumping to conclusions can therefore easily fan the flames of crisis and jeopardise the crisis worker's good efforts.

Consequently, crisis workers would do well to:-

a) ensure that the pressure of crisis does not lead to panic-based false assumptions or a failure to make necessary checks;

b) be sensitive to the possibility that crises are founded on, or aggravated by, misinformation, misunderstanding or false assumptions;

2. Pathologising

One of the aspects of 'new' crisis theory introduced in Chapter 1 was a widening of the traditional focus on individual coping skills to include an understanding of the part played by wider social forces. This wider focus prevents us from seeing simply an individual 'pathology', a person who has failed or is inadequate. It helps to avoid falling into the trap of 'blaming the victim'. (Ryan, 1971)

When a crisis occurs, it is the culmination of a range of psychological and social circumstances and forces putting excessive pressure on a person's (or a number of persons') homeostasis. To concentrate on one dimension only (the individual) and blame the crisis on his or her failings, foibles or fecklessness, is to oversimplify a complex situation.

This process of blaming the victim amounts to 'pathologising' that person or persons. The individuals concerned are responsible for their actions and thus contribute to the crisis matrix. However, we perceive a distorted picture if we see only the dimension of the coping behaviours of the individuals concerned.

The wider picture is represented diagrammatically on the next page.

All three aspects are important as they are part of a complex interaction. We all have a coping repertoire, however limited or extensive this may be. Similarly, we all have some degree of support and we are all exposed to stressors of varying degrees. However, we should recognise the differential distribution of stressors and supports. For example, oppressed minorities face greater stressors - poverty, discrimination, hostility etc. - and yet may, at the same time, have fewer supports to draw upon - lack of money, community organisations, accommodation etc. Thus the combination of the two may place excessive pressure on the third - the coping repertoire. In fact, the coping skills of a person who frequently experiences crisis may be more advanced than another more privileged person, who is more sheltered from the stressors associated with social problems and has a powerful network of support.

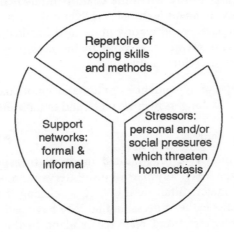

Crisis workers therefore need to beware of pathologising clients by reducing the three elements to one as this is unfair, unhelpful and discriminatory.

3. Creating dependency

One of the primary aims of crisis intervention is to maximise the positive potential of crisis by facilitating the learning of new and better coping skills and the development of support networks. Thus, it is geared towards avoiding dependency and enhancing independence. Ironically, however, the net result can often be a degree of dependency as a result of the process of intervention going wrong in some way.

Dependency can arise in the following ways:-

i) The social worker may do too much *for* the client and not enough *with* him/her. Crises can be severely disabling, especially in the early stages, and doing things for clients is often a reality. However, they then need to be 'weaned off' this as soon as practicable.

ii) Clients can develop an emotional dependence on the worker by becoming over-fond of him or her. Going through a crisis together can form a close and strong emotional bond. Workers need to be wary of the dangers of too close a bond as this could make termination of the case extremely difficult, painful and counterproductive.

iii) If the social worker uses a task-centred approach, the task may be achieved successfully when the client is motivated by the social worker's involvement (extrinsic motivation). If the task does not become sufficiently motivating in itself (intrinsic motivation), the worker's withdrawal may result in the cessation of key tasks. Dependency therefore ensues.

These 3 examples of dependency - pragmatic, emotional and motivational - are serious dangers in crisis work and notable pitfalls to avoid.

4. Closing the door

Crisis intervention is a time-limited mode of therapy. Therefore termination, which is a key part of any intervention, is particularly significant. A major pitfall here is that of 'closing the door'. This entails giving clients the impression that they have had their ration of social work time, effort and resources and no further help will be offered even if very much needed. This can be very demoralising and saps confidence.

This situation can arise chiefly in two ways: either the worker can sow the seeds of doubt by withdrawing with undue haste, or there may be a misunderstanding on the client's part in which it is assumed that social workers deal only with crises.

I have already stressed the importance of terminating intervention effectively. The pitfall of 'closing the door' is therefore a major obstacle to achieving this. Helpful steps in overcoming this would be:-

- gradual withdrawal (although not unduly prolonged), with an emphasis on reinforcing coping skills;

- ensuring support networks are in place and operational;

- above all, making it clear to the client(s) that the door remains open for further intervention, where appropriate, whether on a crisis or preventative basis.

5. Not seeing the wood for the trees

One of the common criticisms of social work is that it is too narrow and individualistic, that it cannot 'rise above a series of cases' (Mills, 1970). In crisis work this is a particular danger, because the social worker is geared towards determining and resolving the specific problematic areas which have provoked, or which are sustaining, this particular crisis for these particular clients. It is therefore understandable that there is a tendency to focus on what is specific to a single case rather than extrapolate the similarities and patterns across cases.

Intervention skills 6 and 7 should go some way towards avoiding this pitfall. That is, applying theory to practice helps to raise awareness of the underlying patterns of crisis and this limits the need to 're-invent the wheel' for each case. Anti-discriminatory practice also draws attention to the shared patterns across cases, the commonalities of oppression and disadvantage amongst women, for example (Hanmer and Statham, 1988).

Good practice in crisis intervention entails both analysing the specifics and locating these within the broader framework of commonalities. A practice which fails to see the wood for the trees aligns itself with traditional crisis theory and all that this entails (see Chapter 1).

This is by no means an exhaustive list of pitfalls. Hopefully it will raise levels of awareness of common dangers and potential errors and hence help to sensitise practitioners to the hazards of crisis intervention.

However, I would not wish to paint too negative a picture, as if crisis work were nothing but hazards. The emphasis in Chapter 2 was on the positive potential of crisis and this applies equally to the worker. There is considerable potential for very effective, successful and rewarding social work. It is my hope and intention that the practice guidelines I have presented here - principles, skills and pitfalls - will tilt the balance in a positive direction by facilitating the development of a theory-based, anti-discriminatory crisis social work.

I shall now move on to look at some examples of such crisis intervention in action. So far, I have sought to update and expand crisis theory, to underscore the positive dimension of crisis and to explore the practice base of the assessment and intervention phases. Chapter 5 builds on these developments by presenting three case studies of crisis resolution. It is to these that we now turn.

Chapter 5

Crisis Resolution

Introduction

The aim in this chapter is to build on the principles, skills and theory base already highlighted, by exploring practical examples of crisis intervention in action.

The main content of the chapter comprises three case studies of social work practice carried out on the basis of an explicit crisis intervention approach. The three cases are actual examples of work undertaken by a social worker. No elements have been changed, except for a few minor details and the names used, which are suitably disguised to maintain confidentiality. Two of the cases derive from a social services department's district office setting, whilst the other relates to a specialist multi-disciplinary drugs team.

The format for each case study is as follows:-

i) Scenario

ii) Assessment

iii) Intervention

iv) Discussion

These case studies are intended as actual illustrations of crisis intervention. Their purpose is to 'bring the theory to life' by allowing links to be drawn between the theoretical concepts and the practice issues which emerge from the cases.

Case A

i) Scenario

The Davenport family were referred to a busy intake team in a social services district office by their health visitor, as a result of child protection concerns.

The family consisted of Mr and Mrs Davenport, aged 23 and 20 respectively and their 17 month-old baby, named Jane. The couple had married six months before Jane's birth and subsequently moved into rented accommodation. They had previously been living with Mr Davenport's parents.

The marriage was a hasty one precipitated by the pregnancy. The couple had only known each other for three months. Despite this, the health visitor had no concerns about the family until the paternal grandparents expressed their anxieties about bruises they had noticed on Jane.

It was at this point that a referral was made to social services.

ii) Assessment

In response to this referral, a social worker visited the family and explained the concerns raised. Initially, Mr and Mrs Davenport suggested the bruising was caused by their pet dog 'jumping up' at Jane or by her self-inflicting the injuries with a rattle. However, they then admitted they were responsible for the injuries and were prepared to accept ongoing help.

In accordance with the child protection procedures, a case conference was held and the decision was made to place Jane's name on the child protection register. Work began with the family to assess the situation and plan intervention.

Soon after this, a further injury was detected by the paternal grandparents which, after medical examination, proved to be a hairline fracture of the child's femur. Again, the medical evidence did not match the parents' explanation. At this point it was felt necessary to apply for a place of safety order in order to ensure Jane's safety. An order was granted and Jane was placed with foster parents.

In some ways, it could be argued that the social worker's intervention, by 'breaking up the family', had provoked a crisis. There was clearly threat involved in the crisis but there was also opportunity, not least to assess the circumstances surrounding the abuse and seek a constructive way forward.

The social worker's assessment highlighted a number of significant issues:-

a) The family experienced a number of crises (including 'life-crises') within a short period of time:-

- marriage
- childbirth
- setting up home independently
- the removal of the child from home.

b) Social work intervention was essential in order to begin a process of change to capitalise on the constructive energy generated by the reception into care crisis.

c) The place of safety order had removed trust, but it was important for this to be built back up again.

d) Jane needed to remain in care until the reasons underlying the abuse could be understood and danger factors removed or controlled. It was necessary to act quickly in order to prevent the situation from 'drifting'.

A picture was painted of a family who were finding it difficult to cope with a number of new experiences, to the point where control was lost and Jane was injured. The impinging pressures included:-

- lack of experience of independent living (including the financial pressures involved);

- a relationship which developed very quickly to marriage and parenthood without having the opportunity to mature;

- very high expectations on the part of the paternal grandparents.

It was important to give the parents space by listening and reflecting feelings, especially the anger they might feel about the situation. Overall, this allowed them to feel safe with the social worker. It worked especially well when the worker was able to reframe the anger/frustration as fear and concern for their child.

As the trauma of the current crisis unfolded, the emphasis moved from immediacy to appropriate planning and intervention.

iii) Intervention

The aim of the parents throughout was to have their child returned. However, this had to happen within a framework of appropriate change/movement by the family and an acceptable degree of safety for the child. It was not simply a matter of returning to the status quo.

A short-term focused intervention was drawn up by the worker and Jane's parents. After some negotiation, a programme of six counselling sessions was agreed. It was geared towards the following areas:-

1. Jane's future.

2. The factors underlying the injuries.

3. The marital relationship and respective roles.

4. Family pressures.

5. Parenting skills.

6. Mutual interests and the development of the relationship.

During this period and beyond, it was agreed that one goal was to maintain contact with Jane and the foster parents.

This was readily achieved and succeeded in developing a close relationship with the foster parents. This was advantageous to the process as Mr and Mrs Davenport became more confident with Jane while in a protected learning environment. The energy produced by the crisis gave them a keenness to learn and to get to grips with their problems. Equally, this paid dividends in the counselling sessions as they were more relaxed and felt supported. This enabled them to deal with the negative dimension of the crisis - the anger, the loss and the sense of failure.

Each counselling session produced different insights and issues which would begin to help communication between the couple.

In session 1, issues around a baby's needs were explored (e.g. shelter, warmth, food, drink, stimulation), and who could and should provide these. This moved into how relationships develop and how important bonds are formed. The role of the father in this was emphasised so as to avoid the development of stereotypical gender roles which would thus place undue pressure on the mother in her role. In addition, there was some movement away from a view of children as possessions, to the respect a child has a right to expect from his or her carers.

In session 2 the parents were able to discuss the injuries and how they occurred. A picture emerged of the practical and emotional problems they had encountered and it became clear that the financial pressures of setting up home, with a young child, on a low income had seriously exacerbated the situation.

Both parents felt uneasy with their relationship and their responsibility as parents. They were quite frightened and had become reliant on outside advice and guidance on how to cope. This produced a double bind: they felt they could not cope without social supports, and yet this felt like failure as the grandparents gave them the message that 'we coped all right with you when you were Jane's age' - they were left feeling unskilled and inadequate.

It became clear that Jane was a child who produced some anxiety in her parents in that she had feeding problems (she was lactose intolerant), which in turn affected her health and sleeping patterns. This tended to produce a vicious circle. This was the framework of events in which the injuries occurred.

However, the combination of support from family meetings, skills training from foster parents and supportive couples counselling allowed an atmosphere of honesty and openness. The parents experienced a process of empowerment and confidence building. Strands of these issues permeated all six sessions and allowed the parents to recognise the factors leading up to the injuries, and gave insights into how, as a couple, they could function best when communication channels are opened up.

During and following the sessions, the parents' contact with Jane increased to the point where weekend home leave was arranged. The foster parents took an active role in supporting Mr and Mrs Davenport and gave feedback on their progress throughout this period.

Ultimately, Jane was placed back home, initially subject to a supervision order, but this was revoked some months later as the parents were clearly coping very effectively. They had come out of the crisis stronger and better able to cope with their pressures and knowing where to get support if they needed it.

iv) Discussion

In this case there was not one crisis but a culmination of several. Each seems to have compounded the next until the situation necessitated outside influences in order to bring matters under control and produce positive change.

Early and intensive intervention and assessment were crucial in allowing the parents to use the situation constructively. In this way, the reception into care became a gateway to solutions rather than simply an additional problem.

It was important for the social worker to frame the intervention in such a way as to help the family appreciate the positive potential of the situation. The subjective dimension - the parents' perception of the events - was as important as the objective dimension.

The parents were able to enter the exit phase in a spirit of seeking empowerment. This would not have happened without the application of counselling skills - listening, reflecting, reinforcing coping skills, etc. Also, clear plans gave structure and boundaries to the clients and worker, and thus introduced an element of control into a situation in which control had been lost. The boundaries produced an arena in which it was felt safe to express emotions - anger, frustration, happiness and so on. But the focus was not simply on the psychological dimension of feelings; attention was also paid to the social dimension of support systems.

Short-term interventions in complex child protection cases can be anxiety-provoking for workers. As in all crisis situations, it is important that the risk involved is carefully analysed. Obviously, in Jane's case this was an ongoing assessment - a recurrent process of 'hypothesis-testing'.

However, it was a positive process which allowed movement and reinforced progress by providing constructive feedback and allowing supportive relationships to develop (e.g. between parents and foster parents and between parents and grandparents).

The most important element of this case was the significant progress towards empowerment through new and effective coping methods and the development of a system of support.

A great deal of thought, time and effort went into this case and clearly not all cases would merit this amount of commitment. However, this heavy investment was justified by the very positive results achieved, thus illustrating one of the key principles of crisis intervention - that intensive short-term work is a 'stitch in time' that saves extensive long-term work.

Case B

i) Scenario

Dawn Weston was referred to the social services department by her GP. The initial request was for a mental health assessment by an approved social worker. Both the GP and the consultant psychiatrist felt she needed to be admitted to hospital on a compulsory basis as she was suffering from severe post-natal depression.

Dawn was 26, as was her husband, Ron. Rachel was their first child. The family lived in a terraced house which they were buying with the aid of a mortgage.

The pregnancy had been an unexceptional one and the actual birth, although two weeks premature, presented no complications. However, on returning home from hospital with Rachel, Dawn became suddenly and inexplicably depressed. She became withdrawn and uncommunicative. She insisted on staying close to Rachel but made no attempt to care for her or meet her needs in any way. It was Ron's concern about this which led to the GP's involvement which in turn led to a visit by the consultant psychiatrist. Both doctors felt hospitalisation was necessary and duly completed medical recommendation forms for admission under Section 2 of the Mental Health Act 1983.

ii) Assessment

After discussing the diagnosis and general situation with the two doctors, the approved social worker (ASW) made a home visit.

An interview with Ron revealed that he was very concerned about Dawn but had no explanation for her sudden and drastic change of behaviour and mood. He was not aware of any difficulties or pressures which could have precipitated the change.

An interview with Dawn initially produced quite a negative response. She seemed to be assuming that the ASW was there to receive Rachel into care. She therefore needed considerable reassurance concerning the status and purpose of the ASW's visit.

Despite pressure from the GP and consultant to arrange urgent admission, the ASW decided to make a further visit the following day.

This tactic paid dividends as Dawn was much more responsive this time. Although depressed, she had realised, largely as a result of the ASW's prompting, that she had reached the 'point of no return' - crisis point. She had realised, perhaps, that hospitalisation and separation from Rachel (the hospital had no child care facilities) were imminent, and therefore she was more receptive to help.

It soon became apparent that there was a serious problem in terms of the presence of Dawn's parents. When labour commenced, Dawn's parents had arrived to 'help out'. They installed themselves in the spare bedroom and set about organising the new baby's environment.

This appeared to have triggered off a re-emergence of problems previously experienced but never resolved. As a child, and especially a teenager, Dawn had felt dominated by her parents and, in particular, by their strict religious views. Dawn had responded to this by leaving home at the earliest opportunity (at 16). This caused her parents great pain and dismay and led to considerable conflict. For several years they were ashamed of their 'tearaway' daughter (as they saw her) and this made Dawn feel both guilty and relieved - guilty about the pain she had caused but relieved to be away from their oppression (as she saw it).

When, a few years later, Dawn became engaged and then married, relations with her parents improved significantly, especially as Dawn was able to keep them at arm's length and not let them take over.

However, just as Dawn was adjusting to the 'life-crisis' of Rachel's arrival, unresolved feelings and issues in relation to her parents were brought rapidly to a head by their attempts to 'help', i.e. by taking over Dawn's household.

Dawn, in her weakened physical state, felt unable to cope with the combination of pressures and felt unsupported by her husband who, she felt, had colluded with her parents. This situation had produced a crisis, to which Dawn responded by becoming depressed - the energy generated by the crisis was turned inwards as depression.

iii) Intervention

Dawn felt as though she had lost control; once again her life was not her own. It was therefore necessary to help her regain control, to take charge. This was accomplished by the following steps:-

1. Dawn's parents were persuaded to pack their bags and return home. It was put to them that Dawn needed more time to herself to sort her feelings out. They were initially reluctant to comply with this, but the authority inherent in the ASW role was perhaps enough to persuade them to accept the advice.

2. Ron arranged to take time off work to be with Dawn and to contribute fully to caring for Rachel. Dawn's earlier comments about Ron had suggested that, whilst he fully wished to be helpful and supportive, his traditional views about the family and gender roles had erected barriers. The crisis, however, appeared to have enabled Ron to break down some of these barriers and to take on caring tasks he had previously seen as not being within his domain.

3. Three counselling sessions were offered to Dawn and Ron with the aim of clarifying/resolving:-

    a) Dawn's feelings towards her parents.

    b) Dawn's religious and moral views. (It had emerged in discussion that Dawn rejected her parents' views but had not developed her own to replace them.)

    c) The need for Dawn to remain in control of her life and Ron's role in helping her do this.

    d) The marital relationship and, in particular the respective gender roles.

As it turned out, because so much progress had been made between sessions 1 and 2, only two sessions were needed. The ASW argued the case for holding the third session as planned in order to consolidate the gains made. Dawn and Ron, however, were adamant that this was not necessary.

These steps were successful in bringing Dawn out of her depression by establishing the balance she needed - the balance between being in control on the one hand, and being supported on the other. She commented that this was the first time she had achieved such a balance. Initially, her parents had been 'overcontrolling' and thus provided too much support, but when she left home she had regained control but felt isolated and unsupported.

Her marriage to Ron had brought her close to that balance but, as she had not shared her views about her parents with him, he had little understanding of her need for such balance. Indeed, until this crisis, Dawn had not articulated within her own mind her problems with her parents. She had just felt smothered and confused, and yet guilty, but did not understand why. The crisis counselling had taken her this major step forward.

The intervention was successful in a very short period of time and produced a very satisfactory and very rewarding end result - a clear example of the positive dimension of crisis.

The positive outcome was largely dependent on the assessment of the situation as a crisis rather than as a medical problem requiring hospitalisation. Indeed, hospital admission could easily have compounded the problems.

The process of intervention was not without its problems, however. For example, the consultant psychiatrist on learning that the recommendations for compulsory admission were not being effected, expressed considerable concern, questioned the ASW's professional judgment and declared that the ASW would be held personally responsible if Dawn were to harm herself or the child. The psychiatrist at this point gave the ASW no opportunity to explain the rationale behind the intervention and was only marginally more willing to listen after the event.

Despite this lack of multi-disciplinary understanding, crisis intervention had been very effective in empowering Dawn and had enabled her to swap hospital admission for the balanced life she sought.

iv) **Discussion**

Many of the characteristics of crisis intervention were visible in this case. Again, the subjective dimension was important, control played a central part and empowerment was a central aim. It was, in many ways, a classic example of crisis intervention, the disciplined application of crisis theory to a crisis situation.

A worker less attuned to crisis theory and its principles may have 'missed' the crisis nature of the situation and may thus have dealt with the case at face value by facilitating the admission to hospital of this 'sick' woman. The fact that there was a clear biological dimension to the situation (hormonal and other changes associated with childbirth) could easily have seduced the worker into perceiving it as a predominantly medical one and thus hospitalisation as the logical solution.

The logic of crisis theory, as we have seen, leads to a very different solution. This does not mean that hospitalisation is never the solution, but it does mean that the implications of admitting a person in crisis to hospital must be very carefully thought through.

There were other significant aspects to this case, the part played by gender, for example. Whereas traditional crisis theory pays minimal attention to structural issues such as class, race/ethnicity and gender, a modern anti-discriminatory form of crisis intervention needs to be sensitive to such issues and take them fully into account. Fortunately, in this case, both Dawn and Ron were receptive to discussing issues of gender and were able to recognise the part stereotypical gender expectations had played in the development of the crisis. Clients are, of course, not always so receptive, for the influence of patriarchal ideology runs strong and deep. However, crisis is characteristically a time when people are more receptive to change than is generally the case.

Values also featured in this case scenario, in particular religious and moral values. One's values are an important source of support in times of stress - a degree of consistency and solidity when all else appears under threat. However, when it is one's values which are themselves under threat, the risk of crisis becomes significant.

In Dawn's case it was confusion over her values which had contributed to her being plunged into crisis. She felt she had not developed her own set of values - what values she had were largely a contradiction of her parents' values, a negative image of someone else's values rather than a positive set of her own.

The combination of the life-crisis of childbirth (in which the responsibility for another human being raises value questions) and the re-imposition of her parents' influence (and thus values) was sufficient to plunge her into crisis, to overwhelm her coping resources. It was the meeting point of the existential dimension (values, meaning, identity, purpose) and the social dimension (power, influence, control, conflict). It was at this point that Dawn floundered but, through effective crisis intervention, was later empowered. She emerged from the crisis a far stronger person than when she had entered.

Case C

i) Scenario

Richard and Sue Parry presented themselves to the Community Drug and Alcohol Team on the recommendation of their GP who had recently become very concerned about Richard's excessive drinking and the effect this was having on the marital relationship.

The team was a small, multi-disciplinary unit with a high workload but a strong commitment to high standards of therapeutic work. Cases were sometimes dealt with jointly by two workers but, at the time of referral, work pressures prevented this happening in this case. The case was allocated to the social worker in the team, supported by consultation with the other team members, a community psychiatric nurse and a psychologist.

Richard and Sue were both in their early thirties, both in relatively well-paid employment with quite good prospects. They had both been married before and Sue had two children from her previous marriage. The foursome lived in a bungalow on an estate close to the city centre.

The couple had only been married a few months and, on assessment, the relationship appeared somewhat fragile and in need of consolidation.

They recognised that they had reached crisis point - they could not cope with the situation as it was - and so they were keen to accept help and to co-operate with plans made.

ii) Assessment

The social worker's assessment soon established that Richard's drinking had only become problematic in recent months. He had been a 'social drinker' since his late teens, but there had never been any concerns about the amount or frequency of his drinking.

The recent pattern, however, was doubly worrying insofar as consumption had increased significantly and had also become secretive. He had tried to conceal from Sue just how much he was drinking. Sue, however, realised all was not well; Richard's tendency to secretiveness implied a lack of trust and thus placed great strain on their relationship.

They realised this could not go on; the situation had become untenable and they felt desperate. Sue felt hopeful but Richard felt helpless to change, but he did recognise that the problem was his to a large extent.

The social worker set about looking for the trigger of the over-reliance on drink (based on the view that the problematic drinking was an attempted solution to an as yet unidentified problem, i.e. the drinking was an unhelpful and destructive coping response). The aim was to identify the underlying factors so that intervention could be geared towards developing alternative, less destructive coping methods.

The couple had had no financial difficulties (although the excessive drinking was changing this). Wider social issues did not appear to be major contributory factors in relation to the problems of this young, white, middle-class and able-bodied couple. However, on closer analysis, both class and gender did have parts to play.

A fragile relationship had been identified by the worker. Although now both 'professional' people, they had come from different class backgrounds with different habits and lifestyles. Their relationship was not sufficiently well-established for them to have come to terms with the tensions and conflicts and to have reached a satisfactory compromise.

Gender issues were also a feature of the couple's circumstances. Sue's separation from her previous husband had been difficult and 'messy'. Sue still saw her husband at weekends when he picked up the children for access. This made for a tense and fraught situation, with confusion over roles and relationships.

Sue's method of coping with being trapped between two men was to become bad-tempered and operate on a short fuse. Richard, by contrast, coped with what he saw as a competitive situation by withdrawing and, ultimately, drinking. The couple did not address the issues together and so this lack of communication and sharing heightened the problems they were experiencing.

Richard had tried to be consistent and supportive in his relationship with Sue and the children, but he felt shut out as if he had not been accepted and integrated into the family unit. The frequent contact between the children and their father reinforced Richard's feelings and he had become terrified of rejection.

In a way, his drinking could be seen as a way of 'resigning before he was fired'. By withdrawing into drink, Richard was anaesthetising himself from his pain. But the drinking only added to the problems, and thus to the pain. The situation therefore became intolerable and crisis point was reached - the point of no return, the critical moment when the relationship was on the point of breaking down.

iii) Intervention

In keeping with the time-limited nature of crisis intervention, it was agreed that the couple would be offered eight sessions in order to maximise the positive potential of the crisis by producing constructive change in the couple and their relationship.

The first two sessions were characterised by avoidance behaviour. Both somewhat defensive, Richard and Sue preferred to focus on the drinking and a strategy for reducing it rather than the underlying problems. The issue of avoidance was therefore raised by the worker as the drinking is itself a form of avoidance - an unhelpful coping method.

It becomes apparent that there is a double-bind. After one 'failed' relationship it is important that Sue is not hurt again. She wants Richard to take more responsibility to show how much he cares for her. However, the more he cares, the more she seems to want to reject him. They are stuck.

In the third and fourth sessions the barriers start to come down and the couple move on quite markedly. It is at this stage that the issues of jealousy and the 'unfinished business' of the first relationship are recognised and confronted.

As a result of this, there is a further massive shift when they acknowledge that their attitude of 'the relationship has to succeed' is unhelpful and they begin to confront more realistically the possibility of the relationship failing.

A further significant point to emerge is that of non-verbal communication. Richard needs continually to touch Sue as a way of making sure she still cares, and tends to follow her around. This annoys and frustrates Sue who feels she has no space. Consequently, the worker sets 'homework' - Sue is to be the one who does the touching, but only when she wants to.

Sessions 5 and 6 represent a stage characterised by relief - Richard, because his need to be cared for is better met, and Sue, because she feels more in control and less agitated.

This relief gives the couple the confidence to say what their needs are in the relationship and how and to what extent they could meet each other's needs. They are therefore able to work on a contract which negotiates how they can function better on a day-to-day basis.

This seems to give them the space to talk more about Sue's previous relationship without Richard feeling too threatened.

The final two sessions were used to consolidate the progress made. They continued to test out their newly found freedom to feel safe enough to express their anxieties of being hurt again, but accepting that this is always a possibility. That is, they were learning to cope with the contingency of their relationship - and indeed of any relationship.

They acknowledge that there is still a lot of work to be done to secure their relationship. However, they now have a framework on which to build. They have been helped to gain the confidence they need to undertake this work themselves without outside support - with the proviso of the safety net that further sessions could be arranged if needed.

By the final session, Richard's alcohol intake had decreased remarkably, as was confirmed by both partners. This was accompanied by a stronger relationship, increased coping abilities and an acute awareness that excessive drinking is more of a problem than a solution.

iv) Discussion

This was not a crisis characterised by panic and a sense of emergency. It was, nonetheless, a crisis situation. The couple's coping resources had been exhausted and they recognised they could not go on - the situation could only get drastically worse or drastically better. It was a challenge to the crisis worker to ensure that the latter was in fact the outcome - to use the energy and motivation generated by the crisis to turn threat into opportunity.

Where alcohol abuse in particular, or substance abuse in general, is considered, there is a need for very careful crisis assessment. This particular case was a genuine crisis, but often the artefacts of crisis are present - panic, confusion, a sense of urgency and desperation - when there is in fact no crisis. This is an example of 'furore', a state resembling crisis but without the motivation to change, without having reached the critical moment, the point of no return. Furore is a coping method, a 'flustered' state geared towards attracting attention and support. It is generally an unhelpful coping method and may therefore result in a crisis in due course. However, it is not in itself a crisis.

This is similar to what had happened to Richard. When presented with stresses and problems, he used the refuge of drink as a way of coping - a destructive coping strategy which led to the crisis. The crisis worker's task, as in so many cases (e.g. child abuse), was to facilitate the development of more constructive coping methods and support systems and thus 'ease out' the more potentially disastrous responses.

The intervention succeeded in achieving this in a relatively short period of time. By having such a rapid impact, the intervention did not lead to the dependency associated with some forms of long-term social work. Crisis intervention succeeded in empowering Richard and Sue to the extent that they had no further need for social work intervention. This avoidance of dependency was of particular importance in this case as the danger here was that Richard would fall foul of another form of dependency - dependence on drink. This would surely have ruined their marriage and thus scarred Sue with another 'failed' relationship, thereby leaving both their lives in tatters.

As this case illustrates, the stakes crisis workers play for are high indeed, but so too are the potential rewards in terms of both client outcome and job satisfaction for the workers concerned.

Conclusion

These three case studies have hopefully succeeded in their aim of giving the 'flavour' of crisis theory in action - crisis intervention in the context of contemporary social work practice.

Inevitably the case-studies are not exhaustive accounts and many aspects have had to be left out. It remains so, however, that the cases depicted here reflect and illustrate many of the elements of an approach to social work practice based on crisis intervention.

The examples used here represent a fairly narrow range of practice scenarios to which crisis intervention is applicable. For example, admitting an elderly person to Part III accommodation is compatible with the crisis approach. Such an admission represents a crisis as it involves the client reaching a situation in which conventional coping resources have broken down and a major change is needed to remove the danger inherent in the situation. And, as experienced practitioners in this field know only too well, such an admission can be either a wondrous relief or 'the end of the road' - thus representing both the opportunity and threat of crisis.

The case examples given here are illustrations of the successful use of crisis intervention, but of course there is by no means any guarantee that success will be achieved. There are many factors that may lead to failure; it is important to recognise that crisis intervention is not a 'magic box' to cure all ills.

The number of social work situations which invite a crisis intervention approach are many and varied and it would be an error of major proportions to assume that crisis theory has only a limited range of application.

Of course, these case-studies are not intended as formulae to be followed or as 'model answers'. Effective crisis work is premised on a good understanding of the principles of crisis theory, the development of skills of crisis assessment and intervention and a sensitivity to the common pitfalls to be avoided. Following a formula is therefore not enough.

These issues will be covered again in Chapter 7, but, before reaching that point, the focus moves from examples of 'conventional' crises to a consideration of crisis on a much wider scale, the multiple crises involved in a disaster situation. The use of crisis intervention in disaster work is therefore the topic of the next chapter.

Chapter 6

Crisis and Disaster

In recent years there have been numerous disasters which have attracted considerable media attention, public concern and sympathy. Overall, there have been hundreds of deaths, hundreds seriously injured, plus immense suffering, pain and anguish on the part of the survivors, the bereaved and the local communities in general.

Disasters on this scale are by no means new, but the fact that so many have occurred in such a relatively short period of time has raised public awareness in general and focused the issues for welfare professionals in particular. But what are these issues? How do they affect social work? Is crisis theory a helpful framework for understanding, and dealing with, these issues?

These questions, and what I see as the appropriate answers, form the basis of this chapter. I seek to establish the validity and relevance of crisis intervention as a model for:-

a) the social work response as and when disaster should strike, and

b) emergency planning in readiness for a potential disaster.

I shall therefore consider how aspects of crisis theory apply to actual examples of disaster work and supplement this with discussion of how a crisis intervention model can and should be used to guide and inform the development of an emergency planning philosophy and set of procedures.

What is a Disaster?

The implication of the term 'disaster', in its current usage at least, is that of a calamity or misfortune which goes beyond personal suffering. It tends to imply large-scale and sudden impact with major consequences. In short, it amounts to a crisis writ large, affecting a number of people or whole communities.

The Bradford City football stadium fire disaster and the Hungerford mass shooting are clear examples of this type of disaster. The consequences or 'ripples' of such events run wide and deep.

There are also the so-called 'natural' disasters of floods, earthquakes etc. Here, there is a direct parallel with crisis theory in terms of the distinction between 'situational' crises (fully contingent upon human actions) and 'maturational' crises (some degree of predictability linked to 'natural', in this case, biological factors). Whether 'natural' or otherwise, the effects of disasters are of major proportions and thus a source of major concern.

We could enter into a debate about the precise definition of disaster by, for example, asking questions such as 'How many victims have to be involved before the term "disaster" is applicable?'. This is an issue which social services departments and emergency planning committees will have to address, but it is not a debate I shall pursue here. All the incidents to which this chapter refers are clearly recognised as disasters with no doubt about their status as such. This is not to deny the difficulty of setting the boundaries of 'disaster', but rather to avoid this difficulty for present purposes, in the interests of simplicity and clarity.

Applying Crisis Theory to Disaster Work

In studying the literature relating to disasters and the social services approach, it becomes apparent that 'crisis' is a frequently used word, but the term 'crisis intervention' features far less often; 'crisis theory' is conspicuous by its absence. An explicit use of crisis intervention principles and theory is not apparent. However, implicit references to crisis theory are not hard to find. For example, Simon Baugh, a psychiatrist from Bradford, is quoted as saying:-

> "Finding out who needed help and offering them skilled counselling could pre-empt more severe and long-lasting distress, and those who later developed chronic depression were often those who had somehow been missed or had declined assistance at the initial stages." (Jolley, 1989, p8)

This is a clear example of crisis intervention rather than crisis survival. The emphasis is on positive and intensive initial input in order to avoid the need for longer-term support. It is not simply first-aid, an emergency repair to tide people over the disaster.

Crisis intervention's emphasis on the need for early and intensive intervention is also clearly in evidence in the report of the Hungerford Family Help Unit:-

> *"It now seems generally understood that early help moderates the after-effects of trauma and later serious reactions are more likely to be amenable to treatment."*
> (Lane and Stacey, 1988, p25)

In the case of the sinking of the *Herald of Free Enterprise*, there was a delay in the response of social services which was later recognised as a mistake. Dave Wilkinson of Kent Social Services Department commented:-

> *"We waited to be asked before we became involved... We wouldn't do that again."* (Lunn, 1988, p29)

A prompt response is therefore recognised as a key part of effective disaster work. I shall return to this point below when we discuss emergency planning.

Crisis theory contends that there is little that can be done in the early stages of a crisis in terms of positive intervention - except for simply 'being there', listening and reassuring, laying the foundations for future work. This is also borne out in disaster work. There are several examples on record of a 'pro-active' approach, usually involving sending a letter to survivors or the bereaved offering support. This differed from the usual social work approach - a reactive one which responds rather than seeks.

The pro-active approach nonetheless appeared to be a successful one. In the case of the Piper Alpha disaster, the response rate was over 85% (Tumelty, 1990, p16). For Kent Social Services Department, over 90% responded in relation to the 'Herald of Free Enterprise' disaster (Jolley, 1987, p8). Tumelty confirms the value of offering help in the impact and recoil phases:-

> *"One thing that with hindsight does seem to have been important was that initial contact by letter and leaflet, phone or visit. Even if not taken up immediately many people came back in the weeks and months following and were able to use that contact to approach us."* (1990, p17)

The phrase 'with hindsight' confirms that this was not a deliberate application of crisis theory. It remains fully consistent, nonetheless, with the tenets of crisis intervention.

When a major disaster occurs, there is much work to be done in minimising the harmful effects - psychological, social and economic. Such work is clearly reactive, geared towards 'picking up the pieces'. It may therefore seem strange to refer to it as *preventative*. And yet it *is* preventative - in direct parallel with the preventative nature of crisis intervention. Work carried out in response to a crisis prevents longer-term distress and disorder. As Anne Bone, leader of the Piper Outreach Team, puts it:-

> *"In my opinion much of the work we have done with individuals has made their trauma a little easier to bear and hopefully in some cases prevented them becoming long-term statutory child care or mental health cases in the future."*
> (From an internal Social Work Department document, Grampian Regional Council.)

Other aspects of crisis theory are apparent in the leaflet 'Coping with a Major Personal Crisis' circulated to people affected by the Bradford City fire disaster in 1985 (and also used, in modified form, in response to later disasters).

The opportunity for growth and positive potential of crisis are reflected in the comment: "Remember that the pain of the wound leads to healing. You may even come out wiser and stronger."

The 'incompetence' associated with the recoil phase of crisis is also recognised with the warning: "Accidents are more common after severe stresses," referring, as we saw in Chapter 1, to the risks involved in e.g. using machinery (Caplan, 1961).

Thus, it is clear that crisis theory has played a part in forming, guiding and informing the social services response to disasters in recent years. Tom McMenamy, Director of Social Work for Dumfries and Galloway, reinforces the central role of crisis intervention when he says of his department's response to the Lockerbie disaster:-

> *"It made me realise how much social work is an organisation for crisis intervention."* (Barry, 1989, p23)

However, what is also clear is that the use of crisis theory appears somewhat hit and miss, stumbled upon as if by accident rather than clearly and carefully thought through as part of an emergency planning strategy. The implications of this will be considered later.

Having considered some aspects of the overlap between disaster work and the day-to-day use of crisis intervention, let us now turn our attention to some of the ways in which disaster work is different.

Probably the most significant difference is the sheer magnitude of the situation. Dealing with a person or family in crisis can be very demanding for the social worker but when this is magnified to the extent where perhaps hundreds of people are involved, the overwhelming pressure on staff should not be too difficult to imagine. Peter Hodgkinson (1988) captures the intensity of such disaster work in the following powerfully expressed passage:-

> *"Disaster work is about being AT THE EDGE OF THE ABYSS. It is a GLIMPSE INTO HELL, not your hell but what could be your hell. It is about the containment of horror, terror and grief that might only otherwise live in our nightmares.*
>
> *Whilst many of us deal with awful things in our everyday work, we have respite from it. The stress is dose-related. A disaster worker literally lives, sleeps and breathes death continually."* (From a paper presented at the First European Conference of Traumatic Stress Studies, Lincoln)

Workers can be surrounded by chaos and extremes of pain and distress for sustained periods of time. Even those workers who are extremely well-equipped in terms of coping resources can find themselves severely tested by the extreme demands of the disaster situation.

Conventional support systems may also cease to apply and thus leave workers with only very limited support. For example, the intensity of the situation may leave no time for supervision or consultation - just at the time when it is needed most.

Although crisis intervention work in general has little respect for office hours, the worker has at least some degree of control over hours worked, regular breaks, time-out etc. In a disaster situation, in the early stages at least, the work demands are such that control over working hours and conditions can be extremely limited. This can, of course, add significantly to the stress levels experienced and the harm done, psychologically and socially, by such stress.

Thus, one of the characteristics of disaster work is a lack of control, a certain feeling of powerlessness, helplessness - factors associated with stress and depression (Davison and Neale 1986, Seligman, 1975). In this way, social workers (and other 'helpers') are particularly vulnerable and run the risk of becoming additional psychological victims of the disaster.

Taylor and Frazer (1981) refer to rescue and support workers as potential 'third-level victims' (secondary victims being the relatives and friends of those mainly affected). Dudasik (1980) refers to such people as 'entry' victims, those who enter the scene later but are nonetheless affected by it. (Both classifications are discussed in Raphael, 1990, Chapter 9.)

Additionally, administrative and support staff involved in keeping records etc. may also be affected by the emotional strain of the disaster, especially as they will not have the same level of experience of dealing with distress as social workers or other professional staff.

A potential 'fourth level' victim can be the organisation itself. Social work agencies can become overloaded by the sheer weight and volume of demand placed upon them at short notice. It is not only individuals who need support from others around them. Social work organisations also require assistance, for example, from neighbouring authorities or kindred agencies.

Crisis workers constantly face the risk of being plunged into crisis themselves (O'Hagan, 1986) due to the demanding nature of crisis intervention. However, the situation depicted here is very different: support systems may be absent, control over the situation is far less than in day-to-day crisis work and the sheer volume and intensity of human suffering and torment is likely to be overwhelming.

A further pressure normally absent from crisis intervention work but starkly present in disaster situations is the spotlight of the media, the glare of publicity.

As Brazier (1990) puts it:-

> "There is nothing new about media interest in disasters great
> and small. They are the very essence of the dramatic headline,
> the front page story and the in-depth investigative follow-up.
> What is now giving cause for concern is the sheer numbers of
> media personnel that turn up and the complexity and
> sophistication of the communications equipment they bring
> with them." (p4)

The sense of shock and chaos surrounding a disaster can be heightened
and intensified by the influx of large numbers of media staff. But press
interest is not only at the initial point of disaster - the weeks and
months of aftermath are also potential sources of 'good stories'.

The involvement of the press is not something social workers usually
relish. Over the years social work has had something of a 'mauling'
from newspapers in general and certain newspapers in particular. The
media presence is therefore likely to be an unwelcome one as the
potential for being misrepresented adds to the significant pressures
already faced by social workers involved in disaster work.

The "Media Factor" (Diment, 1989) is therefore a potential source of
additional stress for disaster workers. However, it should be noted
that the impact of the media on clients can also be a detrimental one.

Anne Bone of the Piper Outreach Team (the team set up in response
to the Piper Alpha disaster) comments on the intrusiveness of some
members of the press:-

> "The public want human stories and the majority of journalists
> are sensitive and provide accurate reporting. Those who do
> not, cause extreme distress which only adds to the trauma. It
> seems that now some of the latter have even posed as social
> workers to gain entry to homes. One survivor agreed to be
> interviewed by someone from the Social Work Department
> only to read his intimate details two days later in a newspaper"
> (internal document 'Press and Media').

The media dimension of disaster work therefore needs to be carefully
handled.

A further aspect of disaster work which differs from that of mainstream crisis intervention is the unpredictable nature of disaster in terms of time, location etc. Social workers wishing to gain experience of crisis work will not have long to wait before suitable work situations arise. However, disasters are less frequent and less predictable and the opportunity for building up expertise is a hit-and-miss affair. It is therefore highly unlikely that the workers involved in any one disaster will have had previous experience of disaster and they will probably have had no training either. Duckworth (1987) comments:-

> "...although disasters appear to occur quite regularly when viewed from a national perspective, any group of helpers is unlikely ever to become 'practised' at dealing with them. In every disaster situation, there will in fact probably be a majority of professional helpers present who, whatever their prior experience, will never before have encountered death, suffering and devastation on such a scale." (p26)

One significant implication of this is that the wealth of crisis experience and expertise available in social work agencies may be lost if links cannot be drawn between such work and the unfamiliar terrain of disaster work. It is therefore important to understand the similarities and differences between crisis and disaster.

One possible solution to this lack of experience is the establishment of a national team available on standby to be introduced to the disaster scene as a matter of urgency as and when required in whatever part of the country a disaster may strike. This is parallel to the American concept of a 'Go Team' which can be mobilised at short notice as, for example, in the Hurricane Hugo disaster in 1989 (Zealberg, 1990). Brook (1990) comments that this was a recommendation put forward by Bradford social workers after the football ground fire disaster there in 1985.

If this, or a similar solution, is not adopted, then it seems likely that there will be one of two outcomes, neither of which offers much appeal:-

1. Massive resources will need to be poured into training large numbers of people across the country on a 'just in case' basis. Given the financial climate in which social work currently operates, the cost of this option would be a major drawback.

2. Social workers will continue to run the risk of being caught up in a disaster situation having had little or no training, briefing or experience. The possible traumatic effects on unprepared staff and the risk of poor, ill-informed practice make this a distinctly unattractive proposition.

Whatever the approach adopted and whatever the training offered to support it, it seems likely that crisis theory will play at least a part in the development of a social work response to disasters.

This, in turn, leads to a further difference between crisis work in general and disaster work in particular, namely the possible need for longer-term intervention. Crisis intervention is geared towards avoiding the need for long-term work by investing heavily in the crucial early stages of intervention. However, the massive scale of disasters means that, for many, longer-term problems can result from the way in which the overwhelming pain and distress of the disaster quickly exhaust the support systems and helping resources available.

Post-traumatic stress disorder is a term used to describe the longer-term psychological harm that can be caused by the emotional impact of a disaster. Davison and Neale (1986) describe the syndrome as follows:-

> *"... a traumatic event or catastrophe of the worst order, such as rape, combat or a natural disaster, brings in its aftermath difficulties with concentration and memory, an inability to relax, impulsiveness, a tendency to be easily startled, disturbed sleep, anxiety, depression, and above all a psychic numbing."*
> (p 138)

In addition vivid flashbacks or 'intrusive thoughts' can trigger off the initial painful and desperate feelings. However, we should be careful not to confuse common post-disaster behaviours with a clinical disorder. Raphael (1990) warns that post-traumatic reactions should not be equated with post-traumatic stress disorder (PTSD). Hysteria, confusional states and even brief psychoses are known to occur in the short-term but quickly clear up. They are transitional states and are not therefore signs of a deep psychological disorder. It is only when such problems persist over time that the term PTSD becomes applicable.

Gersons (1990) links PTSD with crisis theory when he describes the disorder as 'heterostasis', a term borrowed from stress theorist Hans

Selye to refer to an 'abnormal equilibrium'. That is, the effect of the trauma is so great as to prevent a return to a satisfactory level of coping, to 'homeostasis'. Gersons goes on to argue that crisis intervention is not sufficient, as PTSD identifies the additional need for long-term therapy.

There are many techniques and approaches used to tackle PTSD (Rosser, 1990) but groupwork remains a popular choice. Social work has a strong groupwork tradition and so could potentially offer a great deal to the people affected by this syndrome.

Thus, it can be seen that there are both similarities and differences between mainstream crisis intervention and the more specialised area of disaster work. Crisis intervention has a significant role to play in the social services response to disasters; however simply uprooting conventional crisis concepts and applying them to disaster work is not enough. Understanding crisis intervention is a necessary condition for high quality disaster work, but not a sufficient condition. Crisis theory offers a useful framework for disaster work; it now needs to develop and keep pace with the progress of the emerging discipline of disaster theory.

Brook (1990) bemoans the tendency for recent disaster work to be based on 'received wisdom' rather than research or evaluation. He comments:-

> "As a consequence, practice is anchored to an unreliable knowledge base which takes account of neither the complexity of the relationship between disaster and its consequences, nor the uniqueness of each disaster situation nor the limitations of social work as a profession." (p11)

There is a long, established tradition of crisis theory, research and evaluation which can be drawn upon and applied to disaster work. The foundations are already laid and are there to be developed.

Emergency Planning

The next question we need to address is:-

How can crisis theory contribute to the emergency planning process?

Let us look at the various aspects in turn.

1. The Social Work Role

It is helpful here to draw a distinction between social work and social services. The latter refers to a wide range of services provided by Social Services Departments (Social Work Departments in Scotland) whereas the former refers to a narrower range of activities carried out by professional social workers. Walsh (1989), in his study of emergency planning, recognises the role of social services in providing "rest centres, and personnel with invaluable experience in dealing with social emergencies, essential in any relocation exercise, together with supplies of emergency clothing and bedding." (p88)

Clearly social services have a part to play in the immediate post-disaster period, for example in organising supplies and transport. However, there is little emphasis on planning for the aftermath of disaster in terms of the social work role. For example, Walsh's chapters on 'Multidisciplinary Teamwork and Communication' and 'The Psychology of Disaster' make no reference to the social work role.

Kent Social Services Department, in a report on the Herald of Free Enterprise Disaster, also comments on the lack of thought given to these issues:-

> "A retrospective view would cast doubts on the role of the social services as laid down in the Emergency Plan and indicate a more proactive stance for the Department in the care and welfare of survivors, injured and the bereaved as their prime role - rather than that of solely providing rest centres."

Similarly, Tim Lunn (1988) argues that emergency planning had failed to identify clearly a central role for social services in the Dover, Hungerford and Kings Cross disaster situations.

There is a clear message here that emergency planning needs to address the question of psychological and social needs in addition to the now conventional emphasis on physical needs, such as shelter, food, etc.

There is a parallel here with crisis theory's emphasis on the need to understand the major psychological and social impact a crisis can have on an individual, family or group of people. In day-to-day crisis work, social workers can be attuned to such issues by becoming experienced in crisis intervention techniques and crisis theory principles. However, as was noted above, it is unlikely that such experience and knowledge will be readily available in the context of the different demands of disaster work. It is therefore important for emergency planning to take account of these aspects of preparation.

2. Briefing and Debriefing

Disasters produce intense extremes of emotion - fear, terror, grief, longing, anger, bitterness, resentment, guilt, panic and deepest sorrow. The full list would indeed be a long one and the sheer depth and magnitude of such powerful emotions can be overwhelming, and can even rock the very foundations of our stability or sense of self.

For workers who attempt to assist those affected there, is, as was noted earlier in this chapter, a risk of becoming additional psychological victims if the traumatic impact seriously affects them. For this reason, Raphael (1990) focuses attention on the need for workers to receive assistance in the form of debriefing.

It is important for workers attempting to operate in the emotionally highly charged atmosphere of a disaster and its aftermath to have the opportunity to talk about their experiences and feelings - to ventilate and 'unload' some of the pain they have seen and felt.

After exposure to the most negative extremes of human existence - death, chaos, destruction, etc. - it is not surprising that workers in these circumstances will need personal reassurance and some degree of guidance in making sense of their nightmarish experience and somehow integrating this highly distorted reality into the framework of understanding and coping to which they are accustomed. In effect, such workers can be seen to be experiencing an existential crisis in which their fundamental and characteristic ways of relating to the world and their existence within it have been challenged and, temporarily at least, found wanting.

Debriefing can therefore be seen as a means of helping workers cope with their own crisis and come to terms with the anguish and existential trauma generated by the disaster.

The British Psychological Society Report (1990) also recognises the need for workers to have adequate scope for dealing with their feelings:-

> *"Dealing with the victims of disaster raises unusual demands on helpers. Their own personal vulnerabilities and unresolved issues in dealing with bereavement are likely to be exposed. Staff need to be aware of this, need to come to terms with such issues and do need the option of personal counselling, outside of the supervision structure".* (p9)

There are two distinct, yet related, sets of circumstances when the need for debriefing applies. Firstly, workers exposed to the actual impact of the disaster or the immediate aftermath will have particular needs associated with the sudden and acute destabilisation (breakdown of homeostasis) wrought by the overwhelming effects of the crisis situation.

Secondly, there are workers involved in the long process of psychological recovery and rebuilding of communities whose debriefing needs will be different. Their experiences may well be less acute but they nonetheless become exposed to the pain, grief and trauma in a way which is potentially harmful to them. This exposure can go on for months or even years; the negative effects can be cumulative.

Facilities for debriefing, if they are even to approach optimal effectiveness, will need to be planned and prepared in advance. Attempts to construct a debriefing programme in the midst of the chaos of disaster will be seriously hampered if no thought has previously gone into the issues. Where this lack of planning applies, there is an increased risk of workers themselves becoming additional psychological victims.

Similar arguments apply to arrangements for prior briefing in preparation for this daunting work. Training can address general skills and issues, but this needs to be supplemented by specific briefing on the situation which has arisen, the approach to be taken and the worker's role within the plan. Again a great deal of thought will need to be given to the contingency plans and arrangements necessary to facilitate such briefing.

3. Training

Training is commonly recognised as an essential part of developing skills and contributing to making maximum use of the strengths and abilities that workers have to offer. If a local authority or voluntary welfare agency is serious about offering a strong social work response should a disaster occur within or near their operational area, then training clearly needs to be part of the emergency planning process.

The 1989 publication, 'Training for the Caring Business: The Managers' Guide', [1] states that training should:

> *"Enable the workforce, either on an individual or group basis, to develop competencies (skills, knowledge and awareness) directly related to the tasks they undertake."* (p9)

Sending out staff to deal with disaster situations without first having had the opportunity to develop, or even explore, such competencies is to ask a great deal indeed from them.

In many recent disasters, the pattern appears to be one of seeking advice from other local authorities who have mounted a disaster response and/or engaging external consultants to advise. But this has tended to be an 'after the event' response rather than part of preparatory emergency planning.

We should also be aware of Brook's (1990) warning about the use of consultants:-

> *"Caution must be exercised in view of the vested interest they have in selling training and consultation services which they inevitably recommend social work departments to have."* (p.11)

He also goes on to express concern about social work being reliant on private enterprise and argues the case for developing the necessary knowledge base to be able to plan competently for a coordinated and effective service.

The collective wealth of experience and knowledge within social work is vast in terms of loss counselling, crisis intervention and dealing in

---

(1) A handbook published by the Joint Initiative for Community Care/Association of Directors of Social Services/Insight.

general with extremes of despair and suffering. What is needed, therefore, is not a mystique surrounding the area of disaster work, but rather the harnessing of existing skills and knowledge, extended and 'fine-tuned' where required, to form the foundations of a training strategy, a baseline from which to develop.

The insights of crisis theory have a part to play in this insofar as they can help make sense of the chaos and instability associated with disaster and provide a positive framework for intervention. However, as has already been noted, crisis theory needs to be seen as an open and flexible theoretical framework or system; it is not a dogmatic set of 'right answers' to be applied regardless of the circumstances. In this way, crisis intervention can be recognised as a key component in developing training for a disaster response.

4. Existing Workloads

When disaster strikes, massive additional work pressures can be thrust upon social workers, both in the short- term on an intensive basis or a more long-term extensive basis. This in itself provides a heavy and demanding workload but this extra demand is particularly significant when we consider that it has arisen in addition to what is likely to be a full existing workload.

We need to ask: what happens to the high profile child protection cases and statutory child care duties? What attention is paid to disabled or elderly people at risk in the community? In short, what happens to existing workloads?

Much of the routine work will be 'absorbed' in the crisis in a number of ways - when tensions and conflicts are suspended by the drastic effects of the disaster, when client expectations of service are reduced in recognition of the powerful impact of the disaster on the local community.

Much of the work can be 'put on ice' temporarily until at least the immediate aftermath is over. Priority levels will be raised: some will not receive a service who would otherwise have done so. However, there will remain social work tasks which must, or at least should, be carried out.

It is therefore important for contingency plans to be drawn up so that there is at least some degree of clarity as to what should happen to existing workloads and what the hierarchy of priorities is to be. Without such planning there are two clear dangers:-

1. The chaos associated with disaster may distort priorities e.g. a low priority aspect of disaster work may take precedence over high priority non-disaster work.

2. Social workers engaged in disaster work will face additional pressures if they are anxious about the cases for which they are normally responsible, particularly those cases which contain an element of high risk.

This is a direct parallel with crisis intervention work where work systems need to be sufficiently flexible to allow a rapid crisis response without unduly disrupting other important work in progress. This is discussed further in Chapter 7.

5. Potential for Disaster

Crisis intervention is premised on responding to the breakdown of coping resources. Skilled and experienced social workers can often recognise in advance potential sources of crisis, vulnerable weak points in the personal and social circumstances of clients.

This finds its parallel in disaster work in terms of emergency plans being geared towards recognising potential local sources of disaster and initiating preparations accordingly.

Some disasters are more or less totally unpredictable. For example, the Hungerford mass shootings could potentially have occurred anywhere. However, for other types of disaster, there may be some degree of predictability or at least potential vulnerability. For example, some areas such as Towyn will be more prone to flooding than others. In some areas there will be a recognised high-risk location, such as a chemical factory or oil refinery. Factors such as airline flight paths are often taken into account in emergency planning in general, but social work agencies can also gain clues about potential demand for their services should a potential disaster become an actual one.

The greater the risk of disaster in a particular area, the more willing local social work agencies should be to invest in training and planning for offering a good quality social work response to disaster.

Emergency planning is a complex multi-disciplinary subject which is taken very seriously by local authorities. Crisis theory cannot provide all the answers but can make a valid and valuable contribution. In much the same way as crisis theory teaches us to be ready for crises and to be prepared to respond to maximum effect, disaster work needs to be premised on a co-ordinated and well-planned response:-

> *"The most essential element is to have systems and people ready before a disaster occurs. No one can be expected to find out all the data on the appropriate way to manage disasters when they are in the middle of one."* (BPS Report, p5)

Conclusion

Disasters produce a crisis for a wide range of people - direct victims, their friends, relatives etc., disaster workers and members of the local community. Although disaster work is by no means a direct parallel with mainstream crisis intervention work, the fact that so many crises are generated means that crisis theory and crisis intervention techniques can play a significant part in preparing for, and responding to, a wide range of disaster situations.

Disaster work shares with crisis intervention a positive outlook, a determination to overcome adversity and seek out the positives. Disaster is a major existential crisis; it brings home with brutal emphasis the contingency or unpredictability of human existence, the foundations of sand on which human lives are built. From an existentialist point of view, human existence is seen as having:-

> *"... no God-given values, no guarantees and few certainties. It can be a scenario of extreme despair or extreme joy. For social work this is a crucial point. It offers tremendous hope but also demands tremendous effort and commitment."*
> (Thompson, 1990b, p72)

Raphael (1990), in her detailed study of disasters and their implications, also focuses on hope:-

> *"But ultimately, of course, disasters represent on a grand scale the confrontation with death and loss. Thus, for individual and community they symbolise both the cycle of life and the ultimate end.*

> *Survival after disaster symbolises regeneration and rebirth, a*
> *fresh gift of life because death was escaped. Human warmth*
> *and closeness are sought as reassurances of life and sexual*
> *intimacy, and childbirth may result as individual and society*
> *affirm 'we will go on and live'. The renewal and regeneration*
> *of the community convey belief in the future."* (p310)

This message of hope is an important and valuable part of our strategy for dealing with the overwhelmingly negative impact of a disaster. It is this sense of hope which has helped many cope with the trauma.

A recurring theme throughout Raphael's book is the linkage between disasters on a wider, community scale and smaller scale personal disasters, crises of loss and grief of one form or another but experienced at an individual or family level. In short, the macro level of disaster is inextricably linked with the micro level of crisis - crisis and disaster have much in common.

Chapter 7

Implications and Applications

Crisis intervention is a much maligned and often misunderstood therapeutic approach to dealing with people in distress. What this text has hopefully succeeded in doing is to clear up some of those misunderstandings and present a strong case for the increased and more informed use of crisis theory in social work.

What remains for me to do now is to recap briefly on the ground so far covered and then move on, finally, to consider the implications of using the crisis intervention approach within a social work context. Much of the crisis literature relates to crisis work within a medical, psychiatric or multidisciplinary setting. The specific organisational context of social work therefore needs to be considered, for a general understanding of crisis theory will not answer our specific questions about the implications for service delivery.

Exploring Theory and Practice

Crisis intervention refers to the application of crisis theory concepts and principles to therapeutic work with individuals and groups at significant times of acute distress in their lives. I have argued that the term 'crisis intervention' is often misleadingly applied to a strategy of harm reduction geared towards making a crisis as painless as possible. I prefer to refer to this as 'crisis survival' and reject it as a failure to realise the positive potential of crisis intervention. 'Dealing with crises' and 'doing crisis work' are not necessarily the same thing.

I also argued that traditional crisis theory has failed to keep up with developments in social work theory, policy and practice. In particular, crisis theory, as originally formulated, is inconsistent with anti-discriminatory practice. Its focus is too narrow and individualistic/familial to do justice to the impact of wider social, economic and political factors on the 'crisis matrix'. What has been propounded, therefore, is the need to update, amend and extend crisis theory so that it takes fuller account of the sociological dimension of crisis, specifically issues of discrimination on the grounds of gender, race/ethnicity, age, etc.

Similarly, a case was made for deepening traditional crisis theory by incorporating within its framework an understanding of the existential aspects of crisis, i.e. issues of meaning, purpose, anguish and threatened identity. Their absence from early formulations of crisis theory is a significant weakness.

However, despite these gaps and inadequacies, it would be a mistake of major proportions to reject crisis theory in total. The line of argument here is that the immense value of crisis theory is such that it justifies the effort of 'reconstruction' to make it compatible with the strengths of current social work thinking.

One aspect of crisis intervention which contributes to its appeal is its emphasis on the positive. Crisis intervention, as Chapter 2 stressed, is an attempt to maximise the positive potential of crisis, to turn danger into opportunity, threat into growth. In particular, I looked at the applicability of social learning theory as a means of capitalising on this positive potential. However, the beauty of crisis intervention is that it is not 'exclusive', that is, it does not preclude the use of other approaches or therapeutic tools. Social learning theory was chosen as an appropriate vehicle but it is by no means the only one. Many others could have been used. Crisis intervention does not seek to replace other 'tools of intervention' but rather to enhance them, to provide a framework of understanding to guide their use.

A key part of effective crisis intervention is the need for rapid yet accurate assessment. Chapter 3 discussed the principles of good assessment, the skills needed to undertake such work and the pitfalls waiting for us if we are not careful. Figure 1 summarises the issues covered.

A similar approach to the intervention phase was also taken, focusing once again on principles of good practice, the skills required and the pitfalls to be avoided. Figure 2 summarises these.

Having covered the basics of theory and practice, I then moved on to present illustrations of crisis intervention in action. Three case studies were used to exemplify the use of crisis intervention techniques in practice and to flag up important points about the process of applying theory to practice. Hopefully this chapter helped to bring some of the issues to life and thus bring about a better understanding of crisis and crisis resolution.

Figure 1	Assessment	
Principles	**Skills**	**Pitfalls**
1. Early assessment is crucial	1. Listening skills	1. Crisis begets crisis
2. Both the subjective and the objective dimensions must be included	2. Reflecting feelings	2. Moving not at the client's pace
	3. Reinforcing coping skills	3. Seeing a crisis that is not there
3. Assessment should not have a narrow, psychological focus	4. Non-provocative information gathering	4. Seeking consensus
4. Focus on the positive	5. Calming and being calm	5. Seeking certainty
5. Medicalisation should be avoided	6. Time-management skills	
6. The problem focus needs to be delineated	7. Self-care skills	
7. Clear plans need to be formulated		

Recent years have brought something of a resurgence of interest in crisis work due, in no small part, to the large number of disasters in Britain in the latter half of the 1980's. Chapter 6 concentrated on the use of crisis intervention in disaster work. The similarities and differences between conventional crisis work and disaster work were drawn out. Following on from this, crisis theory was used as a basis for understanding some of the issues underlying preparing for a potential disaster response. Of necessity, this chapter cannot be comprehensive but it does set the scene for further work on this subject by drawing attention to some of the important issues.

Figure 2	Intervention	
Principles	**Skills**	**Pitfalls**
1. Delay in intervention tends to be costly	1. Risk analysis	1. False assumptions
	2. Patience	2. Pathologising
2. Intensive short-term work is more effective than extensive long-term work	3. Confrontation	3. Creating dependency
	4. Motivation and self-motivation	4. Closing the door
3. Listening is a key activity	5. Termination	5. Not seeing the wood for the trees
4. A repertoire of methods is available	6. Applying theory to practice	
5. Intervention should be future-oriented	7. Anti-discriminatory practice	
6. Intervention should be time-limited		
7. Crisis intervention is proactive		

In short, what I have sought to do throughout this text is to give an account of the key elements of crisis intervention work in a social work context and with the emerging discipline of disaster work.

Exploring the Implications

We have seen that crisis intervention can be a very effective and rewarding form of social work practice. However, we have also seen that it can be a very demanding and potentially dangerous undertaking.

This raises a number of considerations which should be taken into account. These include:-

1. Dealing with Aggression and Violence

People in crisis can be unpredictable and volatile. Consequently, we need to be conscious of the risk of violence, especially in situations where the crisis worker can be seen by the client(s) as 'the enemy', e.g. child protection cases or approved social worker assessments under the Mental Health Act 1983.

Clients in crisis may feel threatened and vulnerable as a result of the loss which plunged them into crisis and may feel they have nothing further to lose in lashing out. There are numerous cases on record of clients attacking and harming social workers.

Breakwell (1989) writes of 'norms of tolerable aggression' in the caring professions. She argues that there is an expectation that some degree of aggression from clients is inevitable. She comments:-

> *"The caring professions are in the frontline against society's distress and disorder. If the penalties of unemployment and poverty increase, then those who help the poor and the unemployed have to face their frustration and their anger."*
> (p14)

It is precisely at times of crisis when homeostasis has broken down that aggression may overstep the 'norm of tolerance' and becomes unacceptable.

It was argued in Chapter 1 that it is important to see crises in their wider social and political context rather than simply as psychological issues. It is important, therefore, not to see violence as an individual, psychological matter but rather a wider concern. Stevens (1988) comments:-

"The sociological perspective's central premise is that violence can only be understood by reference to the social context in which it occurs. This view, that aggression does not take place in a social or situational vacuum, has gained increasing acceptance in recent years and the consideration of the social context of violent behaviour is of particular relevance to practitioners in the caring professions who deal with social problems as much as individual problems." (p5)

The 'crisis matrix' - the various psychological, social, political and existential factors which contribute to the crisis situation - is to be seen as an important element in our understanding and prediction of violence and our response to it. It is more appropriate to see violence as a characteristic of situations rather than individuals. As Stevens puts it:-

"Bandura, for example, a leading exponent (of social learning theory) has said that in predicting the occurrence of aggression, one should be concerned with 'predisposing conditions rather than predisposing individuals'." (ibid)

Parton and Small (1989) take this a step further by arguing that political and ideological changes brought about by the Conservative Government's programme of restructuring the welfare state have brought about a situation in which there is more emphasis on control and authority and on statutory responsibilities. They comment that:-

"The reason why violence to social workers has become such an issue is not because their clients are inherently more dangerous or that social workers are less able to cope, but because the number of potentially violent situations they face has increased. This increase results directly from changes in the nature of the social work task and the restructuring of the welfare state." (p135)

The same argument could be applied to crises. An increasing emphasis on control and authority manifests itself in, for example, an increase in place of safety orders in place of voluntary care admissions (Frost and Stein, 1989) and thus more fraught, crisis-prone situations.

The links between violence and crisis are also visible in research on the incidence of violence against social workers. Brown et al (1986) found that social work tasks, such as receiving a child into care or admitting a client to hospital under the Mental Health Act powers of compulsion, feature strongly in the violence statistics. And these are precisely the crisis situations in which social workers are involved.

My intention here is not to be alarmist or pessimistic. However, it would be both naive and unfair to paint a picture of crisis intervention which does not acknowledge the risk of aggression or violence. This risk is a fact of life for crisis workers.

It is, however, precisely that - a risk. The majority of crisis intervention cases are undertaken without even a hint of violence and aggression. It is important to put the risk of violence into perspective. Violence is most certainly not a constant characteristic of crisis intervention, far from it, but the risk is nonetheless very real; the threat is always there. It therefore pays to be aware of the risk and be adequately prepared both to prevent aggression overspilling into actual violence and to respond as effectively as possible if it does.

More (1990) provides a useful practical guide and Breakwell (1989) is also a valuable source of ideas. However, it should be remembered that whilst it makes sense for practitioners to be well informed on such issues, the responsibility for coping with client violence lies ultimately with the employing organisation. Social workers are not paid to be attacked. Their employers have a duty to protect them as far as possible and to provide maximum support where such protection fails. As Hopkins (1987) argues:-

> *"Employers are acknowledging their responsibility to minimise the dangers of physical assault on staff but few acknowledge or even understand the deeply distressing nature of the experience and the scars that it leaves."* (p14)

The impact of threat and violence is a significant issue to which we shall return below under the heading of 'Supervision'. Dealing with such matters is an important, if not essential, part of an employing organisation's policy and practice of 'staff care'.

2. Stress Management

Social work has frequently been described as a stressful occupation (NALGO, 1988, Hopkins, 1989), but we need to recognise that crisis intervention in particular is potentially very stressful.

Arroba and James (1987) define stress as one's response to an inappropriate level of pressure. Dealing with other people's crisis can place tremendous pressure on social workers in a variety of ways:-

- aggression/violence (as discussed above);

- feelings of helplessness and powerlessness in the face of overwhelming suffering on the part of a client or clients (e.g. after a bereavement);

- dealing with intense, raw emotion and extremes of distress (e.g. removing a child from home on child protection grounds);.

- unrealistic expectations from clients who see the social worker as the route to salvation (see Raphael's discussion of role stereotypes: Raphael, 1990, p10);

- time pressures - other cases and duties do not disappear while the social worker is immersed in a client crisis;

- crisis is characterised by risk and uncertainty (Thompson, 1990a) and the crisis worker carries considerable responsibility for the outcome of the crisis (e.g. approved social worker assessments).

This is not an exhaustive list but should be sufficient to depict the stress risk associated with crisis intervention.

But pressure is only one component in the complex phenomenon of stress. Another important aspect is that of 'coping resources', the skills, strategies and methods we develop to help us manage the many and varied pressures to which we are exposed. We each have our 'repertoire' of such resources and there are two particular aspects of these coping resources which merit our attention:-

i) Range

The wider one's range of coping mechanisms, the more 'insulated' one is from stress. Where we have only a small number of such resources, we may be vulnerable to being overwhelmed by the pressures.

The range of resources within a person's repertoire can vary significantly. Some people have an extensive repertoire of means of handling pressure - sport, humour, hobbies, a good social life etc. - whilst others may rely on a much narrower range.

ii) Suitability

Coping methods vary in their effectiveness, their timeliness and their 'side-effects' - in short, their suitability for the situation at hand. A method may be suitable at some times but not at others, e.g. humour. Joking at a time of crisis may be helpful or may stoke up the pressures even further. Such situations need to be carefully and sensitively judged.

Some methods are effective in the short-term but may prove detrimental in the long-term. For example, if we deny a problem exists, we are shielded from its pressures for the time being but, in the long run, the fact that we have denied the problem may mean that the pressures increase and multiply until we are forced to abandon denial and confront the problem's existence. In fact, this may actually be crisis point, the time when existing coping methods are ineffective and a new approach needs to be adopted.[1]

Crisis workers, in recognition of the highly pressurised nature of the work, need to be aware of their own repertoire of coping methods and will need to ask themselves two questions of major importance:-

1. Is the range of my coping repertoire sufficiently wide and well-developed to protect me from the pressures of undertaking crisis intervention work?

2. Does my repertoire contain unhelpful or potentially damaging coping methods (e.g. denial, aggression, excessive drinking)?

If the answer to question 1 is no, then care must be taken to extend and strengthen that repertoire. Similarly, if the answer to question 2 is yes, then steps to eliminate or reduce these should be taken so that they can be replaced by more helpful and constructive methods.

---

(1) The notion of denial as an unsuccessful defence mechanism derives from Freud (1933)

One useful step towards achieving the aim of a stronger repertoire is to list or 'brainstorm' the components of one's repertoire and determine which are particularly useful and worthy of nurturance, and which are potentially problematic. If this is done as a group exercise, workers can learn from each other and perhaps identify gaps in their range of resources and pick up useful tips for modifying, extending and improving their repertoire.

A good starting point for considering coping methods is Hopson's (1984) discussion of 'Transitions' and how to cope with them.

The third major component of stress management is that of support, or more specifically, support systems. How well people cope with pressure is not simply a matter of coping methods. It is not simply degree of pressure vying with degree of coping ability. The 'intervening variable' of support plays a major part.

Support systems are of two types, formal and informal. Formal support will be discussed below under the heading of 'Supervision'; we shall restrict ourselves here to consideration of informal support.

Informal support exists both inside and outside work and derives from family, friends, colleagues and other social contacts. It plays a significant role in reducing pressure and reinforcing and boosting coping methods. Hopson (1984) comments:-

> "... interpersonal warmth and support during stressful periods seems to reduce the impact of the stress." (p140)

This statement refers to stressful situations in general but it is particularly applicable to the stresses associated with crisis work. A crisis situation can prove to be a very destabilising experience which unsettles the crisis worker and places a heavy burden on his/her coping resources. Good support is necessary to ensure that the pressure does not overpower the coping resources and produce a breakdown in homeostasis, i.e. a crisis. Good support has the effect of reducing the impact of the pressure and of reinforcing the potency of coping resources. This can be illustrated in diagram form:-

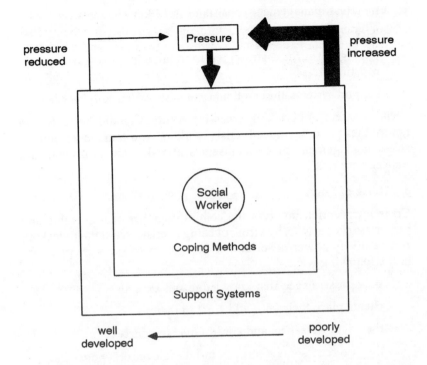

As with coping methods, there are two important questions for crisis workers to ask themselves in relation to support:-

1. Am I receiving sufficient formal support (supervision, consultation, debriefing, training etc.) to help me cope with the pressures of crisis intervention?

2. Do I have access to sufficient informal support (family, friends etc.) to supplement and complement the formal support available?

Where gaps in support are identified, these can be seen as potential weak spots, possible danger signs which should prompt us to take steps to rectify the problem. As I shall argue below, managers have considerable responsibility for ensuring adequate formal support is provided for crisis workers. Informal support, however, is something practitioners of crisis intervention will need to organise for themselves.

In sum, stress management consists of three key elements:-

- 'stressors', the inevitable pressures of crisis work;

- coping resources, strategies for managing pressure and resisting stress;

- support systems, the emotional and practical 'back-up' needed.

Social workers undertaking crisis intervention would be foolish to ignore these issues. Indeed, crisis workers who take no account of stress management place themselves at risk - an additional and unnecessary risk.

3. Abuse of Power

Crisis intervention involves the coming together of vulnerable and powerless clients who, by virtue of being in crisis, are at their weakest, and relatively powerful social workers. Crisis workers are powerful in the following ways:-

- they possess specialist knowledge and expertise;

- clients place their faith and trust in them;

- they have access to, and control over, resources;

- they exercise some degree of influence over other agencies;

- they have statutory powers;

- they have the power to offer support conditionally;

- they have the power to 'close the case' and withdraw support.

Where there is power, there is of course also the risk of the abuse of power. This is especially the case where such power derives from social divisions such as gender, race/ethnicity and age, as these power relations are institutionalised - they are 'built-in' to our everyday thinking and often go unquestioned. (Williams, 1989)

O'Hagan (1986) argues that self-awareness is an important aspect of crisis intervention and I would wish to extend this to incorporate awareness of one's social location and the significance of this in terms of power relations.

If we are to avoid abusing power, it is necessary to be aware of what power we have - in terms of the factors listed above (those deriving

114

from professional status), plus those deriving from one's social location (e.g. the power of men in a patriarchal society; see Rowbotham 1973).

Caplan (1964) makes the point that:-

> *"Crisis... presents care-giving persons with a remarkable opportunity to deploy their efforts to maximum advantage in influencing the mental health of others".* (p54)

We need to be clear that 'influence' is closely related to power. It is a relatively small step from influencing clients to controlling them. Establishing control is a key part of crisis situation but this refers to taking control of the situation rather than control of clients. Of course, there are situations in which control of clients is exercised, e.g. via statutory orders, but this should only occur in clearly defined circumstances and only where necessary.

There is a subtle but significant difference between exercising legitimate authority on the one hand and, on the other, taking advantage of people rendered vulnerable by crisis to manipulate the situation to one's own advantage.

Banton et al (1985) argue that power should not be seen in entirely negative terms as it can also play a positive role. Similarly, Dominelli and McLeod (1989), in discussing statutory social work, comment that a feminist approach may actually be more controlling than conventional methods in order to promote and safeguard the interests of women clients (p112).

This is a complex area with no simple solutions. Influence, control and power are common ingredients of crisis intervention. They can be used positively - within a non-judgmental, anti-discriminatory framework - or they can be abused and exploited, especially in the heat of crisis. One of the implications of adopting a crisis intervention approach is therefore the need to understand, appreciate and guard against the potential for the abuse of power.

4. Supervision

Crisis intervention has implications for the nature of supervision and the supervisory relationship. As we have seen, crisis work can make major demands on social workers in terms of time, emotion, commitment and judgment. Supportive supervision should therefore be an important resource for crisis workers to draw upon. Consequently, it would be helpful to outline what this entails.

One of the tasks of supervision is the provision of assistance and guidance in workload management - to advise on setting priorities and handling excessive workload demands. This task is of particular value for social workers undertaking crisis intervention because of the intensive time demands of crisis work. Crises do not fit neatly into office hours or in between meetings and appointments. A great deal of flexibility is required and the team leader can be called upon to play a significant part in facilitating this.

One of the dangers of poor supervision is that a team leader who is insensitive to (or unaware of) the demands of crisis intervention is likely to add to the pressures rather than subtract from them. It is therefore important for team leaders (and indeed other managers) to have a good understanding of crisis theory and the principles and realities of crisis intervention.

Madonia (1984) focuses on two particular aspects of supervision of crisis workers. Firstly, he comments on the role of supervisors in helping staff who are uncomfortable with crisis intervention methods. Basing his views on his observational research on crisis workers, he concluded that supervisory monitoring was a prerequisite for effective intervention. He comments:-

> "Clearly, these findings demonstrate the strong need for supervisory assistance for those staff who avoid crisis work because of the difficulties involved. Often these workers are capable of working effectively in a crisis setting but, because of the accelerated pace and the acute nature of the problems, supervisory support and assistance are required to help them understand the bases of their reactions to crisis." (p367)

Secondly, he argues that good supervision is necessary for crisis workers in general in order to help skills development:-

> "Worker proficiency in crisis intervention does not happen spontaneously. It evolves during prolonged exposure to work in severe stress situations. Certain administrative and supervisory requirements are also necessary to help workers develop the unique skills of crisis work." (p368)

O'Hagan (1986) supports this view when he affirms that team leaders have a key role to play in helping to ensure good quality intervention in crisis situations.

The pressurised and emotionally demanding nature of crisis work can lead to poor decision-making, unwise moves and a potentially disastrous impact on clients. This is one of the risks of crisis work; those who are brave enough to undertake it deserve the 'safety-net' benefit of effective supervision.

This aspect of the team leader's role acts as a support function for staff. However, there are other support functions which also need to be borne in mind. For example, reference was made earlier to the role of formal support in relation to stress management. Such formal support has a number of dimensions as follows:-

- Shared accountability for work undertaken (thus sharing the pressure to a certain extent).

- The opportunity for constructive release of the intense feelings which can be generated by crisis work.

- Appraisal of performance - constructive feedback on strengths and weaknesses to facilitate professional development and improved morale.

- Team building - helping to provide a supportive peer group and environment.

These are tasks which should perhaps be undertaken in any well-run social work team but, for a team in which crisis intervention is taken seriously, these tasks are key elements in the framework of support. They are an essential component of the support system that gives crisis workers the confidence to tackle crises positively and constructively.

5. Service Delivery Systems

Every social work agency has a system and set of procedures for dealing with new referrals. As with most types of system, there is considerable variation in the efficiency, responsiveness and effectiveness among the different systems in use. As crisis intervention is premised on a fast response to ensure maximum therapeutic value, the system's capability for responding speedily is a crucial feature.

A recognition of this was part of the rationale underlying the development of intake systems in the post-Seebohm boom era of the early 1970s. As Buckle (1981) comments:-

> *"The establishment of intake teams was, therefore, expected to benefit long-term clients by freeing social workers to work more intensely and innovatively with these groups, and to benefit new and short-term clients by dealing with them more quickly, consistently, efficiently and effectively than had been the case."*
> (p44)

The links between intake teams and crisis intervention are long established but, as Buckle goes on to argue (p147) the term 'crisis intervention' tends to be used loosely to refer to dealing generally with crises rather than to a specific theoretical orientation. (This parallells the concept of 'crisis survival' discussed in Chapter I.) It nonetheless remains the case that intake systems are particularly well equipped in terms of being geared towards crisis intervention.

The intake emphasis on fast response provides particularly fertile soil for an approach based on crisis theory:-

> *"Crisis intervention theory, on which intake work is heavily dependent, propounds the view that the early stages of a case are of major significance. It is at such a time of crisis (in the sense of 'disequilibrium') that the energy and motivation required for change are produced. If new referrals have to take their place in the queue with ongoing cases, the crucial early stages can be missed and so other less cost-effective and perhaps less efficacious methods need to be used."*
> (Thompson, 1988, p.21)

However, an intake team system is not essential for good crisis intervention. A well-oiled, carefully thought-out duty system run by committed and experienced staff can also provide the organisational context needed to facilitate crisis work. My aim, therefore, is not to prescribe which system of responding to referrals should be used. Rather, my intention is to advocate that, whatever duty system is in use, sufficient flexibility and responsiveness must be built in to that system to promote, rather than prohibit, good crisis work.

However, we should not allow the emphasis here on duty work to mislead us into the false assumption that crisis intervention is not applicable to longer-term social work cases.

Long standing cases such as statutory child care cases also produce crises and can be amenable to crisis intervention techniques. The service delivery system in which this work takes place should therefore be organised in such a way as to permit, facilitate and encourage the use of crisis intervention.

One aspect of this is the promotion of good teamwork. To allow the flexibility crisis intervention demands, it is helpful for team members to be aware of each other's cases, in outline at least, so that the team can be supportive in dealing with routine work while a particular team member is engrossed in a crisis situation.

One aspect of the organisational context which can help to facilitate this is a 'pairing' arrangement. Each social worker 'teams up' with a colleague and they keep each other briefed on developments in their respective cases. This has three distinct advantages:-

1. If a crisis arises while the social worker concerned is not available, his/her partner will be in a more informed position to respond.

2. As mentioned above, one's partner can help cope with the work left behind when a crisis makes sudden and intense demands on one's time.

3. Pressures and responsibilities are shared by, for example, joint visits or case discussions.

This is only one suggestion amongst many organisational variables which could possibly be changed or adjusted in order to provide a sound organisational context from which to undertake crisis intervention. Crisis work is difficult and demanding enough without having to swim against the tide of the organisational context or culture.

119

Conclusion

This chapter has summarised the main themes and issues covered in this text and thus set the scene for addressing the implications of putting crisis theory into practice. By no means all of the implications have been tackled, but hopefully enough to set in motion the type of planning that has to take place if the major benefits of crisis theory are to be optimally translated into the reality of day-to-day social work practice.

Paradoxically, crises are both usual and unusual. They are, by definition, unusual in the sense that they represent a breakdown of homeostasis, a disruption of routine coping methods. In another sense, however, they are quite usual - especially for social welfare professionals - in that they are frequently encountered. Indeed, for social workers, client crises are commonplace - receiving a child into care, hospitalisation, admitting an older person to Part III accommodation[1] can all be seen as crisis situations. Crisis theory teaches us to understand *both* the specifics of a crisis situation (the unusual), as each crisis contains unique elements, *and* the commonalities (the usual), as the broad trends and tendencies of crisis are readily discernible.

It is at times of crisis that the deepest pain is felt and the full intensity of human suffering can be experienced. It is a time also when human compassion can be most appreciated and most effective. Furthermore, as I have emphasised, crisis is the point at which the potential for growth and enhancement is at its greatest. The art of the crisis worker revolves around helping to guide people from the pain, grief and hurt, through compassion and onwards to growth, opportunity and empowerment.

This text has presented a broad framework and some degree of detail, with the twofold aim of encouraging social workers to tread that path and helping to equip them for the difficult journey ahead.

---

(1) Ratna (1990) bemoans the tendency to exclude elderly people from the purview of crisis intervention. Old age is often (wrongly) seen as a 'contra-indication' for crisis work and yet, he argues, some form of crisis is the main reason for admission to care.

Bibliography

Aguilera, D. C. and Messick J. M. (1986) "Crisis Intervention: Theory and Methodology", St Louis: Mosby

Argyle, M. (1972) "The Psychology of Interpersonal Behaviour", Harmondsworth: Penguin

Arroba, T. and James K. (1987) "Pressure at Work: A Survival Guide", London: McGraw Hill

Banton, R., Clifford, P., Frosh S., Lousada, J. and Rosenthal, J. (1985) "The Politics of Mental Health", London: Macmillan

Barclay Committee (1982) "Social Workers: Their Role and Tasks", London: Bedford Square Press

Barnes, H. E. (1974) "Sartre", London: Fontana

Barry, N. (1989) "Lessons from Lockerbie", Social Work Today, 27/4/1989

Berger, P. L. (1963) "Invitation to Sociology", Harmondsworth: Penguin

Brazier, P. (1990) "How to Handle Media Crush", Civil Protection, No 16

Breakwell, G. M. (1989) "Facing Physical Violence", London: Routledge

British Psychological Society (1990) "Psychological Aspects of Disaster", BPS: Leicester

Brook, R. (1990) "An Introduction to Disaster Theory for Social Workers", University of East Anglia Monographs

Brown, G. W. and Harris, T. (1978) "The Social Origins of Depression: A Study of Psychiatric Disorder in Women", London: Tavistock

Brown, R., Bute, S. and Ford, P. (1986) "Social Workers at Risk", London: Macmillan

Buckle, J. (1981) "Intake Teams", London: Tavistock

Butcher, J. N. and Maudal, G. R. (1976) "Crisis Intervention", in Weiner, (1976)

Caplan, G. (1961) "An Approach to Community Mental Health", New York: Grune and Stratton

Caplan, G. (1964) "Principles of Preventive Psychiatry", London: Tavistock

Coombe, V. and Little, A. (eds) (1986) "Race and Social Work", London: Tavistock

Cooper, C. L. and Makin, P. (1984) "Psychology for Managers", London: Macmillan

Corby, B. (1982) "Theory and Practice in Long-Term Social Work: A Case-Study of Practice with Social Services Department Clients", British Journal of Social Work, No 12

Davison, G. C. and Neale, J. M. (1986) "Abnormal Psychology", New York: Wiley

Diment, D. (1989) "Disasters - the Media Factor", Civil Protection, No 13

Dominelli, L. (1988) "Anti-racist Social Work", London: Macmillan

Dominelli, L. and McLeod, E. (1989) "Feminist Social Work", London: Macmillan

Duckworth, D. H. (1987) "Professional Helpers in Disaster Situations", Bereavement Care, No 6(3)

Dudasik, S. W. (1980) "Victimisation in Natural Disaster", Disasters, No 4

Durkheim, E. (1952) "Suicide: A Study in Sociology", London: Routledge and Kegan Paul

Erikson, E. (1977) "Childhood and Society", London: Fontana

Ettorre, B. (1989) "Women, Substance Abuse and Self-Help" in MacGregor (1989)

Ewing, C. P. (1978) "Crisis Intervention as Psychotherapy", Oxford University Press

Finch, J. and Groves, D. (eds.) (1983) "A Labour of Love", London: Routledge

Freud, S. (1933) "New Introductory Lectures on Psychoanalysis", Standard Edition 22, London: Hogarth Press

Frost, N. and Stein, M. (1989) "What's Happening in Social Services Departments", in Langan and Lee, (1989)

Gersons, B. (1990) "Differences Between Trauma and Crisis: Consequences for Intervention", Paper presented at the First International Conference on Crisis Intervention Approach in Mental Health, London

Getz, W., Wisen, A. G., Sue, S. and Ayers, A. (1974) "Fundamentals of Crisis Counselling", Lexington: D. C. Heath and Co.

Hanmer, J. and Statham, D. (1988) "Women and Social Work", London: Macmillan

Hill, R. (1965) "Generic Features of Families Under Stress", in Parad, (1965)

Hinde, R. (ed.) (1972) "Non-verbal Communication", Cambridge University Press

Hodgkinson, P. (1988) "Managing A Disaster Team", Paper presented at the First European Conference of Traumatic Stress Studies, Lincoln

Hopkins, J. (1986) "Caseworker", Birmingham: PEPAR Publications

Hopkins, J. (1987) "Meeting the Care Needs of Staff in the PSS", Social Work Today, 16/11/1987

Hopkins, J. (1989) "No Words... Just Tears: Stress and Distress Amongst Staff Working in Child Abuse Cases", Child Abuse Review No 3(2)

Hopson, B. (1984) "Transitions: Understanding and Managing Personal Change", in Cooper and Makin, (1984)

Jolley, M. (1987) "Experience of Three Disasters Show Way Ahead to Heal Scars", Social Work Today, 7/12/87

Jones, C. (1983) "State Social Work and the Working Class", London: Macmillan

Lane, S. K. and Stacey, A. (1988) "The Hungerford Family Help Unit", London: NISW

Langan, M. and Lee, P. (eds.) (1989) "Radical Social Work Today", London: Unwin Hyman

Langsley, D. and Kaplan, D. (1968) "The Treatment of Families in Crisis", New York: Grune and Stratton

Lindemann, E. (1944) "Symptamotology and Management of Acute Grief", American Journal of Psychiatry, No 101

Lindemann, E. (1965) "Theoretical Explorations", in Parad (1965)

Looker, T. and Gregson, O. (1989) "Stresswise", London: Hodder and Stoughton

Lunn, T. (1988) "You Bring the Sadness With You", Community Care, 18/2/88

MacGregor, S. (ed.) (1989) "Drugs and British Society", London: Routledge

Madonia, J. F. (1984) "Clinical and Supervisory Aspects of Crisis Intervention", Social Casework, June, 1984

Marris, P. (1986) "Loss and Change", London: Routledge and Kegan Paul

May, R., Angel, A. and Ellenberger, H. F. (1958) "Existence: A New Dimension in Psychiatry and Psychology", New York: Basic Books

Mayes, P. (1986) "Gender", London: Longman

Mills, C. W. (1970) "The Sociological Imagination", Harmondsworth: Penguin

More, W. S. (1990) "Aggression and Violence", Birmingham: PEPAR Publications

Morrice, J. K. W. (1976) "Crisis Intervention: Studies in Community Care", London: Pergamon

NALGO (1988) "Social Work in Crisis", National and Local Government Officers Association

O'Hagan, K. (1986) "Crisis Intervention in Social Services", London: Macmillan

Parad, H. J. (ed.) (1965) "Crisis Intervention", New York: Family Service Association of America

Parkes, C. M. (1987) "Bereavement", Harmondsworth: Penguin

Parton, N. (1985) "The Politics of Child Abuse", London: Macmillan

Parton, N. and Small, N. (1989) "Violence, social work and dangerousness", in Langan and Lee, (1989)

Rachlin, H. (1976) "Introduction to Modern Behaviourism", San Fransisco: W. H. Freeman and Co.

Raphael, B. (1990) (first published 1986) "When Disaster Strikes: A Handbook for the Caring Professions", London: Unwin Hyman

Ratna, L. (1990) "Crisis Intervention: Where it is Contra-indicated", Paper presented at the First International Conference on Crisis Intervention Approach in Mental Health, London

Rooney, B. (1987) "Racism and Resistance to Change", Merseyside Area Profile Group

Rosser, R. (1990) "Planning Psychological Interventions and Evaluating Their Effectiveness", Paper presented at the First International Conference on Crisis Intervention Approach in Mental Health, London.

Rowbotham, S. (1973) "Woman's Consciousness, Man's World", Harmondsworth: Penguin

Ryan, A. (1971) "Blaming the Victim: Ideology Serves the Establishment", London: Pantheon

Sartre, J - P. (1958) "Being and Nothingness", London: Methuen

Sartre, J - P. (1976) "Critique of Dialectical Reason", London: Verso

Seligman, M. (1975) "Helplessness", San Fransisco: W. H. Freeman and Co.

Seligson, B. (1987) "Crisis Intervention: The Concept and Approach of Dr. Nira Kfir", Wendover: Adlerian Publications

Sheldon, B. (1982) "Behaviour Modification", London: Tavistock

Stevens, C. R. (1988) "Violence on Social Workers and The Managerial Dilemma", University of Manchester Monograph

Taylor, A. J. W. and Frazer, A. G. (1981) "Psychological Sequelae of Operation Overdue following the DC10 Aircrash in Antarctica", Victoria University of Wellington Publications in Psychology, No 27

Thompson, N. (1988) "Intake Teams: The Positive Advantages", Insight, 4/10/88

Thompson, N. (1989) "Making Use of Beatnik Thinking", Social Work Today, 10/8/89

Thompson, N. (1990a) "The Uncertainty Principle in Teaching Social Work and Social Science", Social Science Teacher, 19(2)

Thompson, N. (1990b) "Existentialism and Social Work", PhD Thesis, University of Keele

Townsend, P. and Davidson, N. (1987) "Inequalities in Health", Harmondsworth: Penguin

Tumelty, D. (1990) "Lessons of Piper Alpha", Social Work Today, 1/2/90

Walsh, M. (1989) "Disasters: Current Planning and Recent Experience", London: Edward Arnold

Weiner, I. B. (ed) (1976) "Clinical Methods in Psychology", New York: Wiley

Whitehouse, P. (1986) "Race and the Criminal Justice System", in Coombe and Little (1986)

Williams, F. (1989) "Social Policy: A Critical Introduction", Cambridge: Polity Press

Zealberg, J. (1990) "Providing Emergency Care During Disasters", Paper presented at the First International Conference on Crisis Intervention Approach in Mental Health, London.

Index